Everest Canada
The Climb for Hope

Everest Canada

The Climb for Hope

by Peter Austen

With a foreword by Sir Edmund Hillary,
the first man to reach the top of Everest in 1953.

The Caitlin Press
Prince George, British Columbia
1992

The Caitlin Press
P.O. Box 2387, Station B
Prince George, B.C. Canada V2N 2S6

Cover design by Kelly Brooks
Page design by Eye Design Inc.
Cover photos courtesy of Peter Austen and Canadian Press.

Caitlin Press would like to acknowledge the financial support of the Canada Council and British Columbia Cultural Fund.

Canadian Cataloguing in Publication Data

Austen, Peter, 1946-
Everest Canada

ISBN 0-920576-33-8

1. Mountaineering—Everest, Mount (China and Nepal).
2. Everest, Mount (China and Nepal)—Description and travel.
3. Austen, Peter, 1946- I. Title.
GV199.44.E85A88 1992   796.5'22'095496
C92-091506-X

Printed in Canada

*This book is dedicated to
the Rett Syndrome girls
and their families*

CONTENTS

FOREWORD

L ike many people I was not familiar with the problem of Rett
Syndrome but discovered that this disorder may be the most
common cause of mental retardation in young girls. As far as I
am aware, the Climb for Hope was the first time Mount Everest had
been attempted for charitable purposes, and the climb did a great deal
to raise awareness of the Rett Syndrome in Canada.

Although I had no particular connection with Rett Syndrome,
when they invited me to be a guest at their ball and fund-raiser, I was
delighted to join this worthy cause. The Climb for Hope team consisted of climbers from most Canadian provinces. Peter Austen, as leader,
and his team overcame many obstacles on their pilgrimage to Everest:
lack of money, landslides, and terrible weather to name a few. The
attempt on Everest was extremely demanding and the team almost
made the top.

Three climbers reached 26 000 feet but were beaten back by 100
m.p.h. jet stream winds. They were lucky to return alive. The story of
their struggles to reach the summit highlights, by comparison, just
how difficult and heartbreaking the effort to find an eventual cure for
Rett Syndrome will be.

This book is much more than an expedition account. It outlines
the struggle to get to the mountain and to climb it, and it describes it
in an unusually entertaining way.

Climbing can, of course, be dangerous and there is plenty of hard
work and discomfort but it can be fun too. The Climb for Hope was
done to give hope for a cure, hope for effective treatment, hope for
group homes, hope for understanding and support, but above all hope
for the victims of Rett Syndrome.

Sir Edmund Hillary
May 1992

INTRODUCTION

I t was a grey evening in September 1987. My wife Kay, our friend James and I were discussing plans for winter climbing when the phone rang. I had the feeling that it was something important even before I picked up the phone. It was Barry Blanchard, a climber who lives in Calgary and who, like me, had been trying to obtain an Everest permit for years. Excitedly, he said, "Pete, you have permission for Everest; phone the Chinese Mountaineering Association immediately!"

"You're crazy—I've been asking them for six years—Everest's a fading dream."

"Well, the dream's back in focus; get with it."

Could this actually be happening? I pinched myself to make sure I was not dreaming—ouch! How could I phone the Chinese when I only knew two expressions? ni hao (how are you?) and ni hao kan! (you're beautiful!)

I knew a Chinese woman, Mrs. Chow, who lived down the road. I arrived at her door, fell over the step and knocked. When she answered it, I blurted out my mission. She phoned China five times with no results. Excitement was followed by frustration when we heard "yayayayaya" and then "solly"—click.

Finally, a muted voice answered and Mrs. Chow talked to someone in Cantonese. It could have been in ancient Greek for all I understood, but Mrs. Chow was smiling. I was in a frenzy; was it true or wasn't it? She smiled and said it was.

I grabbed the receiver and talked to Ying Dao Sui of the Chinese Mountaineering Association (CMA). We strung together a conversation and he invited me to come to Beijing to meet and sign the protocol or contract. We had been given the time slot of August to September 1991 to climb Everest. Our climb was to be over the Mallory route which has been attempted successfully four times. It had never been attempted in the fall as we would attempt to do.

While that was four years down the road, I knew I had an Everest of obstacles to overcome before ever reaching the base of the world's highest peak. Was I up to this monumental task? I had grown up in England where the tradition of Everest expeditions had originated and where they were a sacred national institution. The few people who had received permission there tended to be part of the establishment. They had had direct connections to banks and major companies that carried on the tradition of sponsoring Mount Everest climbs. The expeditions were usually endorsed by royalty and the British Mount Everest Foundation.

Unlike the British tradition, my path started from scratch, in a part of the world distant from sources of funds, powerful sponsorship or even a tradition of climbing. The expedition turned out to be a veritable magic carpet, a larger-than-life ride through marketing, sponsorship, legalities, and government bureaucracies. There were to be many other, as yet unseen, hurdles throughout the world over the next four years. The major concern was to form a national but cohesive team. It would involve training together at high altitudes, necessitating visiting some very far-flung places.

I had no royal backing—or foreseeable large corporate backing. I, and my three interested friends, had to go pound doors. Once it were known that we were looking for sponsorship, the chairman of the Rett Syndrome Association approached us. After talking with him, we agreed to do the climb for this charity. We were to be the first team to climb Everest to raise awareness of victims of a crippling disease.

The Rett Syndrome is a neurological disease which occurs only in infant girls, and is probably the most common cause of severe mental retardation in girls. When we accepted the Association's backing in 1987, the Rett Syndrome was one of the least understood diseases in Canada. Many in the medical profession had misdiagnosed it. The parents of Rett girls suffered great anxieties and uncertainty, as they watched their daughters deteriorate from about eighteen months onwards. They did not know what was happening. Many wondered if this awful disorder was somehow their fault. Our goal was that the expedition would raise awareness about the disorder as well as dollars for research to combat this terrible syndrome. The team and I undertook every fund-raising vehicle known, plus we invented a few of our own.

For the first three years, we doubted we would ever arrive at Everest. Many expeditions to China are cancelled because of the huge fees the Chinese demand for climbing privileges in the magnificent Himalayas, but our perseverance and sheer doggedness paid off. We were not a "normal" Everest expedition, as we travelled twice round the world. We climbed ninety percent of the mountain, and underwent fantastic experiences and dangers en route. Starting from our initial $10, we raised over $1 500 000. We gained the support of the Canadian and the British Columbia governments. Sir Edmund Hillary, the most famous Everest climber, also supported us.

The preparations for the climb were in many ways more difficult than the actual climbing of the mountain. They occupied the best part of ten years from the time I first applied for permission in 1981 until our summit attempt in 1991. In contrast, our time on the mountain was only three months.

Most mountaineering books deal only cursorily with preparations. They follow the usual format of happenings: get to the mountain, get the camps in, have a go at the mountain. Then go home. All very predictable and unfunny stuff. Our preparations were daunting, complicated and unreal. We had a fascinating cast of characters. Therefore, the story of our preparation is as much a part of the climb as the actual climbing of Everest. Coming from the central interior of British Columbia, we attempted Everest—and we did it to better the lives of Rett Syndrome victims and their families. But it was not an easy task or one lightly undertaken. This book documents it all, from my first application to the aftermath of the actual climb. It includes our high-altitude acclimatisation expeditions to Mexico and Russia as well as our final approach to Everest.

I could spend a lifetime thanking the team, my wife Kay and son Glen, as well as our sponsors for their unfailing support. Those who remained at home did a great job of keeping the media informed of our progress and keeping the information accurate. We succeeded because of them. Λ

CHAPTER 1

The Quest for the Holy Grail:
An Everest Permit

I had discovered mountains in my native Lake District in the North of England, and it didn't take me long to discover the climbing section in our local library. As a child, I marvelled at the early attempts on Mount Everest. The driving force in these early climbs had been George Mallory. This enigmatic and driven man may have made the first ascent of Everest on his third attempt in 1924. But no one knows because he disappeared near the summit. George Mallory and his partner Andrew Irvine were last seen by Noel Odell as they moved up to the rocky section called the "Second Step" at 28 300 feet, high on the north ridge of Everest on June 8, 1924. While Noel watched, the clouds descended around the pair and they were swallowed into the mists.

For Mallory it was the old British tradition of "death or glory." Most modern researchers and climbers think he, in fact, did make the top before freezing to death on his way back down. Throughout the 60s and 70s, I became more and more entranced with the romantic saga of Mallory as I worked and climbed my way around the world. I became determined that, come what may, I would put my own expedition together and try to climb Everest to find out what really happened on that historical, mist-enshrouded June day high on Everest.

Everest has now been climbed from all sides by more than three hundred people. Over a thousand have attempted it, of which a hundred or more have perished. These considerations do not detract from its appeal to climbers. It is the highest mountain in the world, a fact which was disputed for many years. Some people had claimed that K2, a mountain in the Karakoram range in Pakistan, was the highest. However, an Italian expedition in the late eighties did eight readings based on current survey techniques and established, once and for all, that Everest was higher than K2 by some eight hundred feet. While the Everest climb is not technically difficult, the extreme cold, high altitude, avalanche danger, and the willpower needed to climb it make Everest the reserve of the most motivated and— some say—the craziest climbers in the world.

Many people have asked me, "Why can't you just go and climb Everest?" In fact, Bill Tilman, a famous mountaineer and explorer from the thirties, used to say, "You want to climb? Put your boots on and go!" But it's no longer that simple. There are two choices; you climb the mountain from Tibet, which the Chinese insist is in China, or you climb it from Nepal. From both places, climbing the mountain is booked up until well past the year 2010. The trip is cheaper from Nepal, but the dangers of travelling through the Khumbu Icefall— several miles long, hundreds of feet high, and full of huge, horrendously dangerous crevasses or cracks in the ice— make a convincing argument for Tibet.

Obtaining an Everest permit is a full-scale expedition in itself. I had applied to the CMA in 1981 for a permit to climb via the legendary Mallory route. My first step was to have the Alpine Club of Canada endorse my application, a necessary requirement of the CMA. The club readily approved, but getting a reply back from the CMA was difficult. The application got lost. I put a tracer on the registered letter I had sent, but there was no means to track one small missive once it left the morass of Canada Post to arrive in the uncharted wilderness of the Chinese postal system. Finally, I gave up. Then, an envelope arrived with oriental markings upon it. I opened it and a letter, as thin and slippery as British toilet tissue, fell out.

The two lines of the letter said, "Please understand us. Chomolungma is fully arranged until 1998." Two or three readings later, I understood the message to mean that no Everest attempt was possible for us before 1998. Well, I thought, if it were worth a try, it was also worth a second try. I phoned Tom Holzel, a computer design systems engineer, who is one of the world's leading authorities on Mallory as he had led his own expedition to find Mallory in 1985. I wondered if he had any insights into penetrating the maze of Chinese bureaucracy.

Tom was intrigued. He talked to me for over an hour, giving me lots of information about his passion, Everest. After Mallory's death in 1924, Tibet closed Everest until the thirties. Then came three British expeditions, led by the explorer Eric Shipton. Not one reached the top. Then Tibet went secret and closed itself off to the rest of the world.

After the Chinese invaded Tibet in 1950, no further activity took place on Everest. In 1960 a road was built into the base of the mountain and a Communist team climbed to the summit via Mallory's route for the glory of Chairman Mao. Climbers in the West refused to believe that the Chinese had in fact reached the summit because of inconsistencies in the photographic record. However Tom Holzel proved, beyond a shadow of a doubt, by linking certain strategic photographs that the Chinese had reached the top. His research paid off; he received an Everest permit to look for Mallory. rumour also has it that a Russian team of at least twenty men disappeared above the North Col, which is the small pass between the main bulk of Everest and its North Peak. Indeed, we were to find an old rusty Russian ice piton, used for anchoring ropes, half way up the 60-degree avalanche-prone slopes of the North Col.

Tom was very helpful. He suggested we use a Beijing law firm that he knew and that had access to the CMA. The process, he said, would cost $2 000 US and take a year. A year went by and then another six months. The law firm never did manage to pierce the Chinese bureaucracy. I thought, "If this keeps on, I'll be using my old age pension to fund Everest."

We brain-stormed. Why not try the personal touch? In early 1986, I approached Dick Elias, of the Canada-China Friendship Society in Prince George. He kindly made a request to China for permission to climb the mountain. Back came the reply—sorry, fully booked till the year of the dot or the dragon or something. Several of the society's members were going to China a year later. When they arrived they approached the CMA in Beijing with recommendations from the Friendship Society's headquarters in Halifax and Victoria.

Meanwhile, Everest had slipped to the back burner of my mountaineering cooker and I took my family on a holiday to Australia. I had heard of a mystical red mountain 30 000.5 feet high in the north of Queensland. I wanted to find this aboriginal dream-time mountain. In the meantime I was climbing a granite crack on a remote island near the Great Barrier Reef when some thirty feet up, a wallaby jumped out, startled me, and made me almost lose my balance.

This had the effect of making me think, "Good grief—savaged by a baby kangaroo and all these years of careful climbing and gearing up for Everest can be gone in a moment. Your chance for Everest will be gone too." I had a flash of insight that something was going to give.

When we arrived back in Canada, there was a call from Dick that the Chinese had reconsidered and given me a permit for the East Face of Everest, an incredibly dangerous route, 10 000 feet high, which had been attempted only once, unsuccessfully, by the Americans. We could go only in July and August at the height of the monsoon, when the quantities of snow would likely avalanche us off the face of the mountain. I felt a mixture of exhilaration and of that scared uncertainty which mountaineers feel before sticking their necks out on a particularly perilous climb.

I politely wrote back to the CMA, "Thank you very much for allowing us to come and kill ourselves on the most dangerous, unclimbed wall in the world. We prefer to go and play in the traffic in Los Angeles; at least that way we would get to go to Disneyland before we died." I didn't send the letter. I thought our chances for the Mallory route were gone because they had offered us this monstrous wall. However, we played it safe and requested once again, most deferentially, the Mallory route.

More letters and more eloquent appeals later—some six months later in 1987—I received the fateful telephone call from Calgary. Barry Blanchard had been in China and knew first-hand that I had a permit. We were almost in business. Having a permit was fine; what I had to do now was make sure of it. My assurance arrived three weeks after the phone call to China when I received a letter asking for 10 000 yuan, the equivalent of $3 000 Canadian. If we didn't send it within a month, the CMA would assume we were no longer interested and give the permit to someone else. We scrambled to raise the money. Providentially, the Canada China Friendship Society came through with the funds.

After sending the money, I was invited on a fixed-itinerary tour of China. I assumed they didn't want me, an internationally famous mountaineering spy from Prince George, central British Columbia, to find out state secrets on the Beijing streets. To raise travelling expenses, we frantically borrowed money to have T-shirts and sweaters made for a mini-marketing campaign in Prince George and other British Columbia towns.

I had heard that the Chinese are intimidated by taller, bigger people in negotiations. We had also heard of the astronomical prices they charge for their limited services, such as $100-a-day costs per person for spartan room and board. As a result of these factors, I decided to pull out my secret weapon; my very good friend, big Alan Norquay. Alan, at six foot one, is a climber, a powerful cyclist, and a weight lifter. He spends a lot of time talking to his biceps. When he says the right things to them, they self-inflate, and then puff up some more. I knew he would be the perfect back-up negotiator with the Chinese.

We arrived in Beijing on a polluted December day in 1987. Beijing has to be among the worst cities in the world for industrial smog. We had to fight down panicky feelings of near suffocation. Walking through the back streets of the city, we discovered people living, or rather, existing in small two-by-one metre lean-tos. People seemed content to live in this still feudalistic and class conscious state. Communism seems not to have eliminated inequality at all. Everyone knows his or her place and lives in tightly controlled communes. If a person is found guilty of any number of crimes, ranging from consorting with foreigners—which has a variety of meanings—to treason, he/she is taken to a special place in downtown Beijing and executed by a bullet to the back of the head. Then the victim's family is billed for the bullet—or so we heard from residents who dared "consorting" with us.

Another injustice to our western eyes is family size. Legally, families are only allowed one child because of China's population explosion. In some villages baby girls are left out on the hillsides, or so rumour goes. One way round the decree of only one child, we heard, is to make the authorities think the first-born child is mentally handicapped. Otherwise there are heavy penalties for more than one child.

As we walked through a market area, Alan asked me, "Peter, what are those strange skinned animals all piled up on that stall?" Alan is extremely fond of dogs, having two of his own, but I already knew what they were. I had to explain that dogs are cultivated like chickens in China. Al examined his meat very carefully from that point on, especially when it was hidden in sauce.

Cultural differences continued to surprise us. Our official interpreter told us that you don't call women "pretty" in China while the highest male compliment is to be called "tall." For food, we passed up the thousand-year-old duck eggs rolled in clay and the snakes' gall bladders, used to fight arthritis. We did make the first-ever illegal climb of the Great Wall of China and rode on a camel that, I swore, had the same facial expressions as Alan.

While signing the protocol with Ying Dao Sui of the CMA, I watched Al's biceps inflate as with steely eye, he carefully informed Ying that we would fix prices later when we knew what the going rates were. Ying was a fairly reasonable person and all went well. We had a marvellous sixteen course banquet provided by the top officials of the CMA; the only item we couldn't eat was a large green-surely-mutated caterpillar-looking thing which tasted like a large green, mutated caterpillar.

The following night Al and I took our official interpreter Mah out for Peking duck. The six waitresses brought slices but we wanted the whole bird. It took us two hours to eat it. The head was the most delicious part. Unfortunately we had kept Mah away from his commune too long as we drank a wonderful wine called Great Wall Red. His district disciplinarian came and took him away next morning; we figured that the commune official gave Mah a bicycle and a push towards Outer Mongolia.

In negotiations with the CMA, we agreed on how many trucks and yaks as well as how many Sherpas we would need to take from Nepal. After signing the protocol, we had a last look at the Forbidden City, where the Chinese Emperors used to live. The Chinese are somewhat prudish. In the Forbidden City we came to understand the irony of the ever-present curious crowd staring in the window of the Emperor's bedroom, at the bed where his concubines used to frolic.

We left Beijing with permission to climb the mountain, our mountain, Everest. It had taken six years to this point, but I had the feeling we were only just embarking on an adventure that would change our lives irrevocably. ⋀

CHAPTER 2

The Search for Sponsorship

ombing through the fee structure from the CMA, I realised theirs were probably the most expensive services in the world. How in heaven's name would we raise the more than $120 000 that they wanted in addition to the other $300 000 of estimated costs that included transport, food, clothing, oxygen, climbing equipment and insurance? And then there were the costs of the services of the Sherpa guides. I developed bald patches from tearing my hair out, as I worried over the problem of finances.

Deciding that marketing was the key, I approached an international company which specialised in "event" marketing. It tried to discover if Kodak was interested in finding Mallory's camera, a 1924 Brownie. This camera, if we found it, may contain shots of the summit Mallory took before his disappearance. According to some experts, the sixty-seven years of cold would have preserved the camera and film. We then would be able to develop the film on the mountain or bring it back to Canada. Unfortunately, the beginning recession in eastern Canada, combined with the high risk of climbing Everest, was enough to scare away Kodak, even though finding Mallory's camera and pictures of the top would be climbers' equivalent of raising the *Titanic*.

The "event" company bounced out of the Herculean task of promoting us and went back to safe marketing schemes like pogo-sticking around Beirut and day tripping to Venus. We didn't have that option; we couldn't retreat. Alan, James, Timo— another climbing acquaintance—and I formed a society to promote the climb. We applied to the B.C. Lottery Fund after a spokesperson had indicated some funding was available. We were turned down as our expedition was not considered worthwhile by the government of the time. However, we did eventually get written government endorsement of the expedition.

The memory of those days is a kaleidoscope of rejections: National Geographic Magazine said, "It's not American." Chrysler took three months to reject our suggestion of a painted van promoting Everest in the mountain areas of Canada. We approached potential local and national sponsors through the lobbying of people well-known to the sponsors. I asked at least fifty Canadian foundations including Amateur Sport Canada and several in the United States. None would help.

We continued to sell T-shirts and other popular items to underwrite our activities to prepare for the trip. Risky personal loans and donations from friends provided the foundations for our future endeavours. At one point we raffled a boat and outboard and made exactly $9.00.

Then one evening in early 1988 I received the call from Toronto: would I be interested in climbing Everest on behalf of the Rett Syndrome Association? Ernie Sniedzins, the founding chairman, had been attempting to obtain a permit to climb Everest but had met with no success in two years. Later, people asked me later why we had not gone with a more high-profile charity like AIDS or cancer. It is simple: an Everest climb must have a hard-working, totally committed person to run the fund-raising or the climb simply will not happen. Ernie is such a person. He flew from Toronto and showed me a large *Who's Who in Toronto* that he had published as a fund-raiser for the mentally disabled. He was committed to the cause of Rett because his daughter Sarah has been diagnosed with the disease.

We were beginning to rediscover grandmother's saying that the road to hell is paved with good intentions. People wanted to help or said they wanted to help, but the gulf between what they said and what they actually did was often vast. Ernie had promises of sponsorship from people he knew in corporations, but none of these were willing to commit just then. He approached the Canadian government and again received endorsements, which come cheap, but no financial help.

In 1991, four years after our initial sponsor seeking, we had gone through four different ministries and lobbied government departments endlessly. We received, from an assistant deputy administrative assistant to an assistant deputy minister, a token few thousand dollars one week before we left for Tibet.

It was also in 1988 that another climber and business consultant, Jim Everard, joined the team. He approached five hundred companies for sponsorship. Many of them wanted a dollar figure for return on their investment, a factor almost impossible to determine. There is no neat formula to tell business the payback for sponsoring a sport or cultural event. Business does involve a certain amount of risk-taking and sponsorship is one of them. Jim's professional efforts drew a blank at first; however Ernst and Young, the company he worked for, later gave a sizable donation. Jim also managed to get the company to cover the costs of the very important area of insurance. Existing or potential brain damage from living at high altitudes was not covered in the policy, much to the dismay of my family.

Meanwhile, back in Prince George, we were holding casinos and even had an Everest male strip-tease night for which we persuaded the rugged-looking Tim, another recent addition to the team, to perform. He dressed up in the latest climbing gear and took it off slowly and seductively. It was a great success and I would like to say that we pulled Tim from what promised to be a great career as male stripper and bullied him into coming to Everest with us.

When we needed a place to meet, the Prince George Holiday Inn came through. Then we needed letterhead; Spee-Dee Printers helped out. Centurion, a fitness club, gave us free memberships. Pacific Western Brewing donated beverages for our dances. The local newspaper, the *Prince George Citizen*, gave a donation. A local TV station, CKPG, gave us a donation towards training costs as well as a video camera to film ourselves. Legal services and accounting services were also donated. Marge Helminck, an expert with computers, volunteered out of the blue. She had no connection with any of us or with climbing. She patiently took all our minutes and did all our record keeping for four years. She laughed at our crazy jokes which we cracked to keep ourselves sane. She became so much part of the team that she came to Nepal with us and had a great time mountain biking through Nepalese villages.

As plans progressed, we realised that the expedition had to be run as a highly efficient business and that it could only be carried out if we achieved financial stability.

George Mallory's most famous quote occurred when he was asked why he climbed. He replied, "because it's there."

When we climbed, it was a different world. Alan was asked the same question before we received permission. He said, "because it's cheap." This statement was true only if the team knew how to get by on minimal equipment. Even then, we discovered that the costs were growing: telephone, travel, increasing Chinese fees—you name it. Our blueprint for preparation had to be carefully planned and followed. We had to have a plan which indicated the key timing of the most essential elements or risk having the whole trip fall apart. Our level of uncertainty was so high that we should have given up the attempt. We had to persist in the face of recession, shoestring budgets, finely-tuned cost-cutting, as well as constant rejections.

Only an unwavering desire to climb the mountain and to do something worthwhile for Rett Syndrome victims kept us going. While mountaineering on Everest has spinoffs in intangible benefits like teamwork, leadership and international prestige, concrete rewards are hard to define. In our case, however, raising money for Rett Syndrome was a definite, concrete goal even more compelling than the lure of Everest for us unrepentant climbers.

The conservatism of Canadian companies was still not helping us much. Some reasons for non-sponsorship included "Been done before." (Our answer: what hasn't?); "Budgets already committed." (Our unspoken answer: until the year 2035, presumably.) Whatever we requested, a company always had a reason not to oblige. On the darkest days, I would not have been surprised to receive a reply to our request for sponsorship such as: "prefer to sponsor snowgolf team to Siberia this year and tree surgeon lawn mower races in Florida the following year."

We were so frustrated. Mount Everest belongs to everyone. All people have heard of it. Reaching the top is the adventure equivalent of winning an Olympic gold medal. Being associated with an Everest expedition would give a company access to the country's collective pride and the uplift this creates. But the recession and the neo-conservative philosophy had made all companies that we approached risk-shy.

We could not land a major sponsor no matter what we tried. It was costing us all, across Canada, considerable sums in telephone and travel, not to mention costs in lost sleep, cold sweats, and tears of frustration. Meanwhile, in Toronto, Ernie continued to approach many well-known people for public endorsement. By 1989, after two years trying, we had several prominent patrons: the Prime Minister's wife, Mila Mulroney; actor Peter Ustinov, as well as Pauline McGibbon who is past lieutenant-governor of Ontario. Art Egglestone, the Mayor of Toronto, and ballerina Karen Kain became patrons. Reinhold Messner also endorsed us. He is the Italian climber who was the first man to climb all fourteen peaks in the world over 8 000 metres as well as the first man to ski across Antarctica. His achievements still boggle my mind.

Sir Edmund Hillary, the first climber known to reach the summit of Everest and whose fame is worldwide, agreed to be the guest at the first Climb for Hope fund-raising ball in Toronto. A song was specially written for this ball. Kathy McGlynn, one of the singers from the musical *Cats,* sang the song at the ball. The ball's organization involved over 100 volunteers and was a great success. The highlight occurred when all the climbers lined up and did a synchronised chorus line in tuxedos which we called "penguin suits." Two more balls took place in the next couple of years but were not as successful as the first.

In the meantime, in the West, we were busy brainstorming up zany, innovative ideas to raise money. A company which liked the idea of the Everest climb for charity began a monthly newsletter to raise money. Unfortunately it went bankrupt while we were out of the country training, and other creditors got there before we did. As a result, some of our hard-earned cash that we put out as seed money went the way of the dodo bird. A Hawaiian Night in Winter at Powder King Ski Resort just north of Prince George was great fun, but still we were a long way short of the huge sums we needed.

One brainstorm we had for raising money was to put people's names on a computer disc and take it to the summit. To create community interest, we decided to take the Prince George flag. Our attempt at community spirit raised awareness of the trip, but little cash. Local grant applications were also unsuccessful; there was no mountaineering tradition in Northern British Columbia. Very few people or companies were interested in branching out into new promotion activities and climbing, at least from the viewpoint of northern B.C., was very new. Many companies expressed interest but bowed out. Our dream's wings were beginning to resemble the dodo's.

Then in early 1991, four years after we had received permission from the Chinese Mountaineering Association, Cathay Pacific Airways, then the most profitable airline in the world, became interested in our charitable cause. It saw great promotional opportunity in the Everest climb. We received free tickets to Bangkok in return for display of the Cathay logo on our "Everfitness Program" which would reach one million people across Canada. This promotion allowed school children across Canada to climb Everest in their own way by reaching certain standards over limited time periods in their particular sport or activity. For instance, when they had cycled 20 miles this was their equivalent of reaching Camp One.

As there are seven camps on Everest, the school children's Everfitness Program included seven levels. Our camps included Basecamp (BC or Camp One) at 17 200 feet. Here people acclimatise for two weeks. At 20 000 feet is Camp Two, an intermediate camp. Advanced Basecamp (Camp Three or ABC) is at 21 000 feet. This camp is usually reached two to three weeks after initial arrival.

Then the climbers reach the majestic North Col where Camp Four is established at 23 500 feet. Camps Five and Six are established between 23 500 and 27 500 feet. The final camp, Camp Seven, is at 28 000 feet. It is a small camp, a last resting place before the summit at 29 029 feet.

Our despondency lifted. Again we viewed climbing Everest as a trip to the moon on gossamer wings. Compass North, a clothing company based in Vancouver, provided more clothing for the expedition. Associated Grocers of Calgary offered the food for the expedition. "Wonderful," said Alan, "we can now have Red River cereal for every meal," grinning at me. He knew I hated the stuff. In reality, we received all the food we needed.

Certain conditions, however, were still very trying. One, Cathay would only stay with us if our proposed satellite system for emergency use on the mountain was in place. Cathay's name was to be mentioned worldwide twice a day. Such a link-up was a vast logistics and financial enterprise. It would be difficult to orchestrate because a few companies monopolise satellite dishes worldwide. Huge sums of money were needed for back-up systems and insurance. The few suitable dishes were being used to cover the growing crisis in the Persian Gulf. Compass North would only stay on as sponsor if we filmed the expedition as we had proposed. The film grants were anything but certain.

The whole sponsorship system was a lofty house of cards, ready to topple at the slightest breeze or quiver of someone else's uncertainty. If one sponsor pulled out, the others were likely to follow. It was as volatile as the 80s' stock market. Uncertainty continued to threaten our house of cards right up until we actually left for Everest.

We were still sending and receiving faxes right until we arrived in Nepal. Faxes buzzed and slid into trays in Canada, Nepal, Thailand.

We had to come up with money to send our equipment to Nepal and to store it there. Next, we had to pay customs duties for Nepal as well as Tibet. It was an unending parade of costs demanding to be paid right away. Close to $250 000 still had to be covered. Luckily, our main sponsors began to see the expedition as a positive way to raise their corporate profiles. They signed on and wanted returns, reliability and association with world class athletes, which we were sure we were.

In the beginning, I had thought that companies would be wooing us for the right to participate. I always learn the hard way. The final outcome of our effort was that we had most of the equipment, food and travel covered before we left for Everest. Unfortunately, there were still huge cash outlays to be made but no money to cover them. We had to dig deep into our own pockets. However, we were to have many more adventures before we actually left for Everest. One of the first problems was who, exactly, were "we?" $\bigwedge$

CHAPTER 3

The Team

Perhaps the biggest challenge after getting the permit was the colossal task of putting together a team. You might well ask, "How do you put together such a team?" I had briefly considered going solo as I had the ability. However, I gave that idea up almost instantaneously. Climbing this mountain would involve so much personal risk that there was a distinct possibility of never coming back. For a solo climber, there would be no support and no rescue, if they were needed. Others have tried solo. Messner, probably the best climber in the world, is the only person to have climbed the mountain on his own in 1980. Even he was at his last gasp when he staggered back into Basecamp. Another acquaintance of mine, Roger Marshall, fell 1 000 feet to his death on the return from a solo attempt on the north face in 1987.

Everest is an unrelenting, harsh task-master.

I pondered taking the friends I normally climb with, but they had no high altitude experience. Nor did they have much experience of the vast organisational logistics this enterprise called for. Now, however, we can boast after our four years of climbing, manic fund-raising, and related business that any of us could now run General Motors, a McDonald's franchise, play golf every day, *and* go on another expedition every other year.

One of the first questions I faced was the size of the team. We needed, I figured, 12 climbers to ensure the correct support and manpower to get up the mountain; any more and the team would be too unwieldy. Some previous expeditions had up to 100 climbers and 500 porters. *The Ascent of Rum Doodle* by W. E. Bowman contains a very amusing section where he jokes about a climber needing two porters to carry his gear and these porters needing four more to carry theirs, and so on, until there is a vast army of small boys being engaged to carry for the porters. "The boys' mothers were all so glad to get rid of them," he states. I wanted to hire only five Sherpas. These people are the legendary small, wiry, and unbelievably strong mountain people, who emigrated from Tibet to Nepal. They have been helping climbing expeditions for close to a hundred years. Each Sherpa we hired was eventually to cost $8 000 which was paid to the CMA, not the Sherpas. With only five Sherpas, we would have to carry much of the equipment ourselves.

At the start, there were only four climbers. Of these, James Nelson was an engineering draughtsman. Because he worked so hard on organising the expedition, raising two young children as well as paying off a large mortgage, I gave him an imaginary, pet ulcer and christened it "Spot." James is a gentle person with one anomaly: he loved dangerous survival games. For example, one cold January, we made an epic ascent of the 1 000-foot, right-hand side of the Twin Falls in Smithers, British Columbia. It is a spectacular frozen, almost vertical, waterfall. As the snow lay too deep on our planned escape route at the top, we were there for the night. Our sweaty clothes froze solid, and we were on the verge of hypothermia. A fire kept us going, but there was not much sleep. James kept cracking jokes the whole night long even when, very dehydrated, he had to drink a horrible brew from Al's helmet, the only receptacle we possessed. This brew was a delightful blend of snow melted in the helmet over the fire. It was lightly seasoned with bush potpourri of twigs, spruce needles, the sweat from Al's brow, and our imaginations. His humour was going to be sorely tried when James acted as basecamp manager on the Everest expedition.

Another original team member is Al Norquay, a chemical engineer and a tireless worker. He looks like a larger-than-life version of Alfred E. Newman of *Mad Magazine* fame. Alan has a great sense of humour. It would be a definite asset in his job as team manager. Everyone appreciated his no-nonsense approach. Right from the early organisational days, he often worked on his computer until late into the night, sorting out schedules and movement of materials. He never neglected his "dependents," two large German Shepherds, during these planning stages.

A third "original," Timo Saukko, is Finnish. He began climbing on one of my courses in 1986. He progressed rapidly and became a strong, competent climber. He spoke very little, and when he did, it was in semi-incomprehensible English. On occasion, he would talk enthusiastically about his experiences. People would listen and join in his laughter, but when he had finished, they would walk away scratching their heads in puzzlement. By the time the expedition left Canada, we could comprehend about seventy percent of what he said. Timo's task was arranging oxygen supply, an important element. His job required endless coordinating. On climbs exceeding 26 000 feet, artificial bottled oxygen is required. Our team required sixty of these bottles which weighed sixteen pounds each. These bottles were manufactured in England; the regulators in California. Six months before the team's departure for Everest, the bottles were shipped to California, filled with oxygen, and then shipped to Nepal. Timo succeeded at this daunting task.

While these team members were well known to me, I now had to find the rest of the team. I wanted these people to be from all across Canada in order to make this the first truly national team. To forge a team, we would have to climb together and find out each other's foibles in great detail before we attempted Everest. I wanted people who had much climbing and high altitude experience, but low ego levels. As well they would need a sense of fun. They would have to be reliable and incredibly hard-working. Most importantly, I wanted people with whom I could trust my life. I advertised throughout North America and received over two hundred applications. Surprisingly, only two were from women. My home became a hotel for the next three years while the original team and the potential team members got to know each other.

One of our first recruits came by word of mouth. In 1988 my doctor told me about an immigrant South African doctor who would fit the team I needed for Everest. Dr. Denis Brown came to see me. Denis is a fascinating character: he had fought in the Zimbabwe War of Liberation in 1975, had been a policeman in South Africa, has climbed many high peaks, and speaks with an even stranger accent than I do.

He is inexhaustible in the mountains, both in action and enthu-siasm. He has an endearing quality of absent-mindedness which shows itself when I asked him a question. For instance, "Denis, why do you climb?" With a faraway air he will say something like: "Be-cause I love people and mountains and medicine. Yes, I love people and mountains and medicine. What? Oh yes, I love people, mountains and medicine. What?"

Everyone on the fledgling team agreed Denis was the happiest person any of us had ever met. Denis threw himself into the medical needs of the expedition with a strange, absent-minded passion. He was very successful at lobbying medical supply companies. We had enough remedies to cover all known diseases as well as some that still haven't been discovered.

The climb would require the services of two doctors who would alternate between Basecamp and the advance camps high up on the mountain. A doctor was necessary at Basecamp for climbers acclima-tising and for those returning from higher levels. A 14-mile-climb above, a doctor would tend to the needs of climbers returning from attempts for the summit. The two doctors would alternate between the two camps so they would each have a chance to climb.

Many doctors answered my ads, but Dr. Mike Sullivan, a neurol-ogist from Chico, California seemed to have the knowledge and required attributes. He seemed laid-back yet enthusiastic in his let-ters. When I first met Mike, his enjoyment of fast cars and his dan-gerous sport of cave diving in remote places belied his easy-going temperament. He had much experience with altitude-related diseases. Any climber who can stay an unpretentious, committed doctor while dealing with the uncertainties of people's nerves has to have the the attributes needed on Everest. As it turned out, Mike was a valuable team player and we all appreciated his presence.

"Rip," or Tim Rippel, joined the team in 1988 while he was a ski school director and operations manager at Powder King Ski Resort in northern British Columbia. I was impressed with Tim's work ethic, likability and zest for the outdoors. As well, I admired his phenome-nal skiing and climbing ability. He was renowned at the resort for get-ting up at 4:00 a.m. to go ski touring before putting in a 14-hour workday, during which he did the work of three. Tim was not easily flustered on the many climbs we did together but was wildly excited when I asked him to come climb "the Big One."

I first met Michael (Myk) Kurth way up on an icefall in a remote part of Jasper Park in Alberta. He was home for Christmas from his job in Dawson City in the Yukon, but was escaping the hordes of people who lived farther south by climbing in Jasper. Right then I knew he was his own person. He took nothing at face value. He analysed, questioned, and dissected everything before making a decision. Myk climbed, as he said, "because it's fun. It's pure and it relates immediately to the natural environment. It's not a 'conquering' thing. If there's anything to be conquered, it's yourself." Myk had gone solo to the top of Canada's highest mountain, Mt. Logan, in a raging blizzard and returned successfully. However, he was not a team player although he had much drive and ability. I knew he would have to work really hard to fit in with a cohesive team, and he did. On one occasion, he drove 1 600 miles in a weekend to meet the team in Whistler for a training trip. Another time he drove from Hinton, Alberta to Prince George for a fund-raising event.

Alan Hobson is a journalist from Calgary who hounded me for a whole year to join the team. I was skeptical because Alan talked like a high-powered broadcaster, and gave the impression of using people for news and then casting them off. I believed that journalists wrote what their editors wanted and thus distorted the truth. In his favour, Alan is the author of *Share the Flame*, the official retrospective book of the 1988 Olympic Torch Relay. He had also won the William Randolph Hearst Award for excellence in journalism. After several meetings, I came to realise Alan's integrity, sincerity and amazing energy levels. He used to train by carrying 100 pounds in his rucksack and running up the fire stairs of high rises in Calgary. His maniacal expression, strange behaviour and heavy breathing frightened more than one woman office worker on her way to lunch.

At first, because he wanted to convince us that he was a professional, he was a dry stick: too serious by far and too absorbed in the immediate task, whatever it may be. This approach was not too successful with the team because climbers are free spirits and do not take things too seriously except, of course, climbing. After all, we live on the edge much of the time. I use the word "edge" to describe the mental as well as the physical conditions of climbing. As time passed, he relaxed and showed great concern about the other members on the expedition.

To train, he climbed the highest mountains in Mexico, Orizaba, 19 000 feet; and in North America, Mt. McKinley, 20 300 feet. These trips cemented his relationship with everyone. He put in a dogged labour of love to acquire an emergency satellite system to use on Everest at great cost of money and energy to himself. His consistent humanity and good humour were really appreciated by all of us once on the mountain. Choosing the right people is always a gamble and I had to go with gut reactions some of the time. Luckily, Alan was a good bet.

Jim Everard, one of our driving forces in fund-raising, is a management consultant and a former banker. He is also a high achiever, having attended The Johns Hopkins University in Washington, D.C. He had been a lieutenant with the Canadian armed forces but he somehow avoided the military brainwash and remains a free spirit. As he is small, although powerfully built, we billed him as the "small-

Mt. Robson, 13,000 feet.

est and baldest consultant ever on Everest." While training for Everest, Jim completed the Midnight Sun Marathon on Baffin Island more than five hundred miles north of the Arctic Circle.

Jim is a world traveller and one of the most even-tempered people I have ever met. He has a nutty sense of humour; he used to send me articles from the *National Enquirer*: "Space Babies Found on Mt. Everest. UFO Wreckage All Over Everest and What Did the Babies Live On?" "Mountain Climbing Can Impair Thinking, Researchers Warn." Hence we learned why we climbed these huge lumps of clay and why we had been called "Conquistadors of the Useless" by at least one perceptive wit. He was a real asset to the team.

Another well-travelled climber who joined us was Ross Cloutier, a search and rescue instructor with the Provincial Emergency Program in British Columbia. Ross had already been over 21 000 feet eleven times and had climbed Mount Robson, the highest peak in the Canadian Rockies, five times. His rescue skills would be needed on Everest. In Nepal he was a godsend with the paperwork. His talents were pivotal in obtaining sponsorships of clothing and sunglasses. Ross also arranged for a film team to accompany us to document the expedition.

The only woman who came on the trip was Hilda Reimer, the cook. Originally from Manitoba, she had learned mountain skills in the Rockies and had cooked for up to 300 people for two months at a time. We figured as we were only 15 in total, she could cook as before, and we would have the other 285 people's rations.

Ernie Sniedzins, our main fund-raiser, was also part of the team but not as a climber. Ernie is a consummate risk-taker. He left his job with Xerox Canada after nineteen years in order to raise funds for the Rett Syndrome. He funded his own efforts for three years, almost going bankrupt in the process. He was doggedly persistent and would never take no for an answer. He was motivated by an almost superhuman desire to make the world a better place for his daughter and others who have Rett Syndrome.

Ernie approached corporations for four years and just when it seemed he was getting somewhere, the target corporation would find an excuse to back out. He would shrug and carry on. It must have been difficult to maintain his perspective when he was continually rejected. He was the oldest team member and liked to lie about his age which was somewhere between forty and fifty-five.

Dr. Mario Bilodeau is from Quebec. His English is as heavily accented as Jean Chretien's. I first met Mario in Russia while climbing Mt. Communism on one of the team's pre-Everest high-altitude conditioning climbs. There, he helped to save a person's life high up on the mountain, but his unselfishness lost him his chance at the summit.

Mario looks like a black grizzly bear with his barrel chest and full black beard. He is an adventure professor at the University of Chicoutimi, Quebec. He lives only for the outdoors and for passing on outdoors knowledge to others. He is not a pedant, though; he has a gentle, guiding way of teaching. He has worked a lot with mentally handicapped people, so he was a natural for a Rett-Syndrome-sponsored expedition. While many climbers tend to view climbing as the most elite, most prestigious of all sports, Mario avoids such classifications with a passion.

John McIsaac was an operations manager for a construction company in Alberta. Like Alan Hobson, he hounded me for a year before convincing me with his efforts and cheerful nature that he was right for the team. John climbs because, in his words, "it's an inner, personal challenge to keep yourself in control. Too much in life is handed to us. But when you get into the mountains, it's just you and your character. You find out who you are. To come out of it successfully re-affirms my self-esteem." But Everest turned out to be very hard on John.

Jamie Clarke joined the team at the last minute as the assistant communications guru to Alan Hobson. He was the youngest member of the team and I took a chance on him. Really, by this time, I wanted only people I really knew well and trusted implicitly. However, Jamie was new to all of us. He is a cross country skier of great ability who had tried out for the 1992 Olympic team. If he had made the team, his energies would probably have been diverted and he would not have come with us. Luckily, he turned out to be really upbeat, fun loving and hard working. He loved to tease the yak drivers in Tibet. He would be up late into the night using our satellite link up to talk to the folks at home. Although he had little climbing experience, he joined in and helped out where he could. His wise-cracking personality became indispensable in dispelling the some-time tension and harder times of our expedition.

There were many more on our team than just climbers, though. The film team, after the Sherpa, were probably the next most important group of people. One member, Pat Morrow had become the second Canadian to climb Mount Everest in 1982. He was also the first person to climb the seven highest summits on all seven continents— an amazing achievement. His books and photography are world-renowned. Pat is introspective but always ready with a perceptive, witty comment. His many previous excursions into Nepal and Tibet had gained him much insight and knowledge which he shared with us on our odyssey through the East.

Bill Noble, from Vancouver, was our second cameraman. He had filmed in many adventurous situations beforehand but never at this altitude. Bill fitted right in as he was also a climber. Both Bill and Pat were to put in much time carrying equipment on the mountain as well as making a tremendous film which was shown across Canada in July 1992.

Mike Collier is the owner of Yaletown Productions, a Vancouver-based film company noted for its super productions. Mike made the film possible at great financial risk to himself. We enjoyed his crazy sense of humour all the way to Basecamp. There, altitude headaches kept him flat most of the time.

Bob Gibson works for Mike. He directed the firm as far as the Tibetan border, as well as doing final editing back in Canada.

While putting the team together I was trying, as the expedition leader, to discover the best way to understand the type of leadership needed to unite the climbers. It was a difficult task as the team was a mixed bag of personalities, while we needed a compatible and harmonious group. After all, our purpose was the incredibly difficult goal of climbing Everest. I discovered that I would have to change many of my own behaviours to achieve optimum leadership in highly stressful situations. Poor decisions and/or poor leadership could result in death of one or more of the climbers.

To add to the general problems of leadership, climbers are a difficult group to lead. They usually climb in pairs and look after themselves and their partner, as they have an independent outlook. In a large group, they have to make a conscious effort to care about all the other members. This can be a long process to develop.

To understand the demands of leaders in adventures or explorations, I studied famous leaders of exploration, such as Sir Ernest Shackleton, who attempted to cross Antarctica but had his ship *Endurance* crushed in the ice. He took some of his men in three small boats across the storm-lashed Southern Ocean, reaching Elephant Island. At one point they were capsized by a monstrous 100-foot wave. He crossed the glaciers on the Island of South Georgia on foot until he reached a whaling camp. He had been away from civilisation for many months and had been given up for dead. After three attempts, he acquired a ship to Chile. Then he rescued his men stranded on Elephant Island without losing a man. His men would have followed him to the ends of the earth.

On the other hand, Captain Robert Scott, the second to reach the South Pole, was not a great leader, and his leadership decisions were partly to blame for the disaster that befell his party upon returning from that most isolated place on the planet. Whereas Shackleton worked as an equal of his men, Scott was an authoritarian style leader who considered himself to be superior to his men. He made a host of impractical decisions. His expedition took horses to the South Pole, then he put a dog-handler in charge of them. He had too few camps; the expedition was stranded in bad weather.

I tried to avoid mistakes by studying previous problems. Major successes blind people to the potential disasters that "just about" occurred. Therefore I find it profitable to study failures in order to find how to avoid them. Stories of successes seldom include details of nearly-missed disasters. Even so, we were to come close to disaster high on the mountain but managed to avoid it.

I had put together a team of professionals who were also climbers: three doctors, two engineers, two managers, two educators, two broadcasters and four business people. Having this team prepare for Everest and move up the mountain would take astute leadership. Any form of authoritarianism would be anathema. All must be involved in decision making. None of us could afford to harbour hidden agendas; we all had to be open. We would have to be agreed on any course of action. I would have to tell them things I hadn't even thought of yet. I like to think that I put out a challenge, inspired a shared vision, enabled others to act, and modelled the most appropriate attitudes and behaviours. I hope I also showed that I had fun doing so. To climb Everest, I felt I had to have people who shared my crazy sense of humour but would not lose respect for me.

My answering machine sang, to the old "Rawhide" tune, backed up with cow and horse sounds:

"Rollin,' rollin,' rollin,' though the phones are groanin,'
Keep that phone a moanin,' Don't hide.
We're driftin' in the sunset so don' hang up the handset.
Get back to you at the end of our ride."

Some applicants hung up, thinking the message indicated lack of preparedness and an unworkable attitude, but I wanted to talk to the ones who garbled their messages because they were laughing so hard. They also had to have requisite qualifications. My reasoning was a great sense of humour is essential at high altitudes because people get irritable and self-pitying when they have bronchitis or lung problems. A sense of humour was the only antidote.

Leadership is difficult to define. Some say it is the process by which change can be understood and dealt with. That is to say it is a process of guiding yourself and others to accept and handle change. Leadership concerns long term strategies and a constantly changing vision of the world. It involves people on an equal basis. Historically, corporations have always assumed people either possess leadership or they don't; however, I believe it can be nurtured. We all contain the seeds. As the events unfolded, most of my team accepted my approach to leadership. According to my thinking, they had almost total responsibility in their individual expedition functions but still were answerable to the rest of the team.

The main principles of leadership are simple. For example, a survey in the USA discovered that people at an executive level in two hundred companies waste three months a year attending genuinely unnecessary meetings and writing pointless memos. We decided to have quick meetings that addressed the issues, period. Our training trips over the world developed great rapport. The to-the-point meetings and training trips allowed me to quickly isolate the two members of our first-run team who would not be able to fit in the team to finally challenge Everest.

With this final team, I had to watch how I used my power as expedition leader. While power or authority is the basic energy necessary for initiating and sustaining action, I had to use it wisely. I could safely assume all team members had suffered from abuse of power in the past, as just about all people have. How was I to be incisive, understanding, but direct? It was a question to be faced again and again. It was never completely answered.

Power involves mutual influencing. Often the team influenced me more than I did them. Other people had influenced me to turn our expedition into a carefully run business. The people who emerged as lead climbers had cultivated "relationship power;" that is they cared for the others and it showed. If they hadn't had this rapport, their orders would have been opposed by the rest. Supplies would not have been moved—or only with reluctance and frustration—thus sapping the team of energy which would be better saved for climbing Chomolungma.

If power relationships caused stress, I had suggestions:
1. Climb facing outwards—dangerous but great views.
2. Start a nasty rumour and see if you recognised it when it came back around.
3. Leaf through old Geographic type magazines and draw underwear on the natives.
4. If your nose ran and your feet smelled, check to see if you were upside down.

I thought a lot about conflict. It is a nasty issue and some of the team said I did not deal with it very well. I agree totally. A leader needs to know when to hold back, say nothing; suppress the conflict at all costs; or suggest a compromise. It is probably the toughest aspect of leadership. I found that with these intelligent people, the best course was to prevent conflicts completely because they usually got out of hand and caused alienation in stressful situations. When conflict did happen, I tried to reach a compromise through a long discussion. For example, to pull our equipment out of customs in Nepal cost $2 000 storage fees. One team member, Ross, figured we could have bribed our way out of it. I did not. Time was short and this disagreement caused some conflict as the team had to come up with some money pretty damn quick. I compromised, saying that the portents for bribery had not looked good, but we would try it next time. At a later date it did, in fact, work.

At other times, I would take no action about a conflict, preferring to leave it unresolved. I figured it was better this way. People are very unpredictable, no matter how well you think you know them. Even the nicest can bear grudges. If someone holding my rope on a difficult section cares to remember a big fight we have had, he may let me continue to fall if I miss my footing, resulting in serious injury or even death.

Many of our team had charisma, a useful style of leadership if used to raise awareness. After all, we were taking huge risks, physically and financially, and taking on the highest challenge in the world. As the leader, I had to cope with an incredible degree of risk. In fact I had to welcome this risk as an adventure and a challenge. Our team risk and mistake level was unbelievably high. There would be many events, impossible to predict or plan for, affecting our climb. Sponsors

Everest Training on north face of Mount Athabaska in the Canadian Rockies.

would pull out; contracts would not be honoured. The eastern attitude toward life, strange customs, landslides, illness, and danger—all would hold us up. At one point James, the business manager, got his tie stuck in the fax machine and we joked that he found himself back in Canada!

The right leadership got us the team I wanted; it also got us the money and made the climb possible. No one was killed although we had some close calls. If the team and I hadn't worked together, who knows how it would have turned out. ⋀

CHAPTER 4

The Mexican Adventure

exico. What this name once conjured up for me was fiestas, sun, sea, and holidays. At first I did not think it would be good for mountain training, but then realised that there are three really high volcanoes in Mexico: Orizaba, at 18 700 feet; Iztacci-huatl, at 17 800 feet; and the most famous, Popocatapetl or Popo, for short, at 17 200 feet. Members of our team had had a lot of mountain experience but some of them had only been to 10 000 feet. These needed high altitude experience. James, Al, and Timo decided to go for the experience of climbing at the 19 000-foot level. I agreed to accompany them, thinking it would be a routine climbing trip. My family came along too, for the excitement of going to Mexico. Neither Kay nor Glen had any intention of climbing.

Everest is 10 000 feet higher than these mountains, I thought. But then I realised the enormity of the difference. The air pressure at the top of Everest is an eighth of that at sea level. The team had to experience the horrors and rigours of height.

The physical logistics of climbing the Mexican volcanoes are relatively simple in theory. Climbers book a flight to Mexico City, hire an incredibly expensive Volkswagen bus, and then drive to each volcano, stare at the objective for half an hour, and then boogey on up. In practice, however, this does not happen in Mexico. Oh to be so naive! The hurdles were to be many, as we found out in a hurry.

My first inkling that Mexico was not all fiestas was as the plane descended into Mexico City. Through layers of thick, heavy pollution we could but barely make out the vast sprawling city. It was eerie.

Twenty-five million people lived here, a mile above the sea, but the haze of pollution was as great as that of Los Angeles—or greater. The acrid air even penetrated the plane's air system as we descended.

The hotel, recommended to us by supposedly good friends, was almost as bad as those we were to visit later in Tibet. My first glance in the chamber of horrors loosely called the kitchen remained with me for three days. Fortunately, the anticipated "personal volcanic eruptions" did not materialise. Before anyone got sick, we left to visit the famous Aztec pyramids at Tenochtitlan.

We went to a bullfight. A girl came out bravely to challenge a young bull. The bull took one look at her and craftily sidled up to her as she tentatively waved the cape. It moved like lightning and got her. The crowd roared and rose. The experience was totally engrossing but somewhat macabre. A horn pierced her side and the bull lifted her into the air. The orderlies distracted the bull and the girl was taken, bleeding, from the stadium accompanied by applause from the crowd. Their appreciation of her courage was tangible. Then five macho, strutting bullfighters performed. My heart went out to the poor courageous bulls, all condemned to die cruelly by the sword on that hot and humid evening.

Al, for some masochistic reason, wanted to drive through Mexico City, just to say he had done it. Since he was driving, we agreed. We went round one roundabout at least six times trying to find the correct directions. Timo shouted, "There is is!" "No, it isn't. That's the bullfight place."

Traffic signs in Mexico only give a vague indication of direction and we ended up on wild chases all over the countryside much of the time, but we finally made it out of our first "Everest" of the urban scene, Mexico City, in stifling and polluted heat. To celebrate we crammed into a tiny village store to buy beer. I was carrying mine out when the rotten bottom of the beer case gave out and crack! sploosh! —six broken bottles lay on the sidewalk. I didn't feel it was my fault, but the local Mexicans did not see it that way. Sheepishly, followed by a hundred Latin stares, we roared off to the horizon, somewhat rattled.

I was driving and noticed a sign indicating our destination lay in another direction. Ignoring the shouts of everyone telling me not to, I did a fancy U-turn in the middle of a town. Damn. Everywhere it is possible to pull a minor traffic violation in Mexico, there lurks a policeman waiting to pounce.

"Follow me, señor," he said, as he led us off to the local station house, "Americans, huh? Licence, please. Dollars, please." "Let's have ten dollars from everyone or we'll be in jail tonight, possibly forever."

Justice in Mexico assumes that a person is guilty until proven innocent. For the tourists, this means pay up and be gone. Otherwise you could be there forever, just waiting to prove you were in the right. Things are getting better owing to efforts by the government, but the tourists still have to watch their step once they get off the beaten track.

After our bribe, we were let go with the words, "Señor is very generous. Muchas gracias."

I had been worried the police wouldn't return my licence but they did. In Vancouver, police give tickets to cars illegally parked. In Montreal, they use clamp-locks. In Mexico, they remove the licence plates. This effectively stops a person from driving. If someone is caught without the plates, the police can jail him. Driving in Mexico, we quickly learned to always have one person on the lookout for cops. If a tourist has a traffic accident, many people advise that the wisest course is just to vanish. If you do not, so the pessimists say, you can languish in jail until a large bribe comes from home. Luckily we did not have to test this advice. Mexico can be a horror show for tourists as greedy, rapacious "operators" are anxious to trap and bleed the unwary and naive tourist. We learned a lot about naivete on this trip.

At the next gas station the greasy gas jockey charged us double the pump price. Al was about to protest, but then we noticed four cops on the other side of the street, watching us very closely. We smiled at each other and thought, "Forget it." We beamed vacuously at them as we presumed they would enjoy their slice of the surcharge.

Visiting and illegally—but harmlessly—climbing more pyramids enroute to the volcanoes was a fun time. James could not resist the multicoloured blankets and trinkets the street vendors were selling. He only paid a half of what they were asking and thought he had a good deal. Probably they would have been happy with even half of what he paid, but nobody minded.

The Aztec name of the volcano we were to climb first was Popocatepetl which means the "Smoking Mountain." According to legend Popocatepetl, a warrior, loved Iztaccihuatl, "The Sleeping Woman" and daughter of the emperor. While Popocatepetl was returning from a victory in war to claim his beloved, his rivals sent word that he had been killed; she died of grief. Popocatepetl built the great volcanoes that lie southeast of Tenochtitlan as a memorial. On one he placed her body, and on the other he still stands holding her funeral torch. These were the volcanoes we wanted to climb.

The air was clear and cold, well below zero, as we mounted the slopes of Popo in the grey of dawn. We had already wandered around acclimatising for three days. Our plan was to rush for the top and then dash down before anyone got ill. The health problems of climbing come from remaining at high altitudes. However, the sickening sulphur smells just before we reached the rim made us worry about other health hazards.

We definitely were not the first to climb this volcano. In the 16th century, Cortes had lowered men into the crater to mine the sulphur using thin cord woven by Indians. We were fortunate because our ropes were much better. We did not have the same fears of plunging 1 500 feet into the molten, stinking hell which grinned and beckoned at any sloppily placed feet.

The weather was bad; it was the rainy season and temperatures were lower than normal. The struggle from the lower rim to the top took us several hours in the high winds and zero visibility. All the time we could feel the pull of the chemical abyss on the left. "A good simulation for Everest," I thought, "although Everest does not smell like rotten eggs." The snow was frozen hard. We had to take great care in the vile smelling mists to avoid the long "bumslide" to eternity.

Although several of the team were suffering from Montezuma's revenge, we took a backroad to the next volcano, Ixty. We ended up on a road so bad that even an "eight-wheel-drive" would have difficulties. The ruts were as deep as a four-year-old is tall. Brown, sticky Mexican gloop was everywhere. People talk about prairie gumbo; well, this was worse. The slopes of Popo had been frozen, and like the twits that we were, we tried a short cut, thinking the roads lower down would be frozen too. The "push-me, pull-you" mud opera went on for hours;

sometimes we would hold our breath, standing in the gunge, while Al drove and we shouted instructions:

"Left...right...watch it! Stump! Hole! Tree!" and occasionally "Mule!" as we careened on two wheels round blind corners. We would wait around a bend while Al took a run at it. His eyes would take on a hunted look and his big arms would be a blur, as he turned the wheel this way and that, fighting to keep control. This was, after all, the first descent of the Popo backroad in the rainy season and almost as much adventure as climbing. We emerged in Cholula, blinking our eyes in amazement. We had made it! It was probably the thought of not being able to return the rented vehicle and spending "trece años" (thirteen years—a favourite jail term) that had kept us maniacally heaving the vehicle round the bends.

Cholula has a famous pyramid filled with tunnels and we found it fascinating to explore. As usual on our Mexican adventure, there was a down side. The guide told us to give him five dollars each after the tour. It was a totally unreasonable sum. The tour was only about an hour long. There were eight of us. Forty dollars? Even Parks Canada isn't this expensive. I told him in pigeon Spanish to get stuffed. When we arrived back at the van, a sixth sense made me look under the wheels and lo and behold, I found bits of broken glass carefully arranged behind the wheels. Expecting the police to arrest us for sabotaging our own van, we peeled out out of Cholulua in a shower of goop.

Once we reached a higher level, Mexico reclaimed her charm. Ixty or "The Sleeping Woman" was windier and even colder than Popo but the hike up to the tiny alpine cabin at 14 000 feet was truly magnificent. We met a party of students who were there with a guide. They had a whole gallon of home-brewed mescal with the worm in it. The brave drink this with lemon and salt. After the third round they pass out with a benevolent smile.

Taking off the following morning was even harder because of the extreme cold. It was -20°C. Crossing the high glaciers in the dark was nerve-racking, but we reached the top just after dawn in a raging wind. The mountain did not awaken, and there were no eruptions except for ours at one minute intervals at both ends, from constantly eating gloppy prepackaged food.

On to our next volcano, Orizaba, the highest. We followed black smoke-belching trucks for hours to the tiny town hidden away in the countryside. There Señor Joachim Canchola Limon lived in tongue-twisting Tlachichuca, three hours from Cholula. We had heard about his hospitality to mountaineers and hoped he would agree to be our guide to the mountain. He welcomed us at his high front gate and we drove into a self-contained, walled farm which was full of goats, pigs, and cows—all on about a quarter of an acre. He was such an unassuming, charming guy that our hearts went straight out to him.

He looked like Charlie Chaplin and also walked like him. We just needed to give him baggy pants, a bowler hat and stick and start filming the Mexican *Gold Rush*, or more in keeping with his lifestyle, *Goat Rush*. His wife and daughters were smiling, wonderful women. We felt immediately at home.

The amount of postcards adorning his humble living-room testified to his popularity among climbers all over the world. We fed royally on refried beans, salads, and hot Mexican food. Joaquim spent the evening fixing his ancient four-wheel drive in order to drive us to the Piedra Grande Hut at 14 000 feet next morning.

After leaving his friendly compound, we drove through the goop until Joaquim stopped short on a steep section one hour from his house. A piece had come off the back axle. He got out and fell on his knees. A serene expression came over his face.

"This must be serious," said my son Glen with a distinct note of glee.

Visions of struggling on foot with huge packs, for six hours up to the hut haunted us. Joachim prayed for ten minutes and disappeared under the truck. He emerged half an hour later with a delighted expression on his face. He said what sounded to us like: "Feexed, si, si. Fantastico. We conteenyou. No?" When we finally reached the hut, it was drafty and cold, but Joachim regaled us with stories of some of his former clients till midnight.

Setting off at 2:00 a.m., we toiled for six hours up the eerie slopes of Orizaba, the third highest peak in North America. Only Mt. McKinley and Mt. Logan are higher. As we climbed higher, the slopes became steeper and we passed the scene of several fatalities. Conditions were extremely icy and foggy; however, we decided to continue.

This climb woke us up. Until now, we had been playing. Now we were forced to remember mountaineers must stay aware in the mountains and always maintain a healthy fear. Become blasé, lose your concentration, and you are gone.

The snow formations on the summit were beautiful, encrusted frost formations which looked like white pennants. The summit cross glistened and shone. The sky cleared for an instant and the Gulf of Mexico appeared in the distance. James was ecstatic; this was his highest mountain so far. Al's eyes were smiling as he peered out from a snow-covered hood. Timo's beard was a long white icicle.

"We made it, guys."

"Yep. Sure did."

We had climbed the three volcanoes in eight days. We had reached almost 19 000 feet. It was a good building block for the next, much more serious step on the scary roller-coaster to Everest. Russia was waiting for us. △

Mount Iztaccihuatl, not most tourists' vision of Mexico.

CHAPTER 5

Perestroika in the Pamirs

fter Mexico, all the team had been to at least 19 000 feet and
had experienced high altitude conditions. The horrendous
wind of Mexico had been a good preparation for the legendary
bone-chilling winds of Everest. At this point we carefully considered:
should we continue or give up before things got too involved?

What the heck, life's an adventure, anyway, and all the world's a
stage, we decided. We're merely crazy players. But we needed a second act: somewhere even higher and more serious but without awkward logistics. Rumour had warned we would have enough of that
with the Chinese in Tibet.

The Soviet Union seemed perfect. It was fairly easy to get ourselves "invited" to climb Mount Communism, a 25 000-foot peak in the
Pamirs, in Kyrgyzstan. It was somewhere near the Great Silk Road
where the legendary Marco Polo once passed through on his way to
Beijing. We applied to the Soviet Mountaineering Association and
three months later while "Doctor Denis" was walking into my house, I
said: "Hey, Denis, your visa for Russia just came." Denis gasped and
went quiet in amazement. He couldn't believe the Soviets would let
him in. He had a South African passport and they frowned on people
from South Africa.

But it was true; we were all going.

The 99-percent humidity in Moscow was awful.

"There's Myk," I said. I could see him as he towered over the
crowd. Myk was one of those guys who would frustrate a high school
counsellor into climbing Everest to avoid dealing with people like

Myk. He had made it to Moscow only at the eleventh hour, after buying a last minute black market ticket couchette ticket from Paris to Moscow at the Warsaw station. To join us in Russia, he had come from Switzerland where his wife lived. At one point the railway authorities neglected to tell him that he needed a bed to sleep in on long distance communist trains or he simply wouldn't be allowed to travel. Getting around this drawback took an extra day.

Once we were all on the bus from the airport, it broke down and we were towed by another bus the twenty kilometres across Moscow on a luxury sight-seeing tour of uniformly grey Soviet apartment buildings. Everyone went to sleep and the snores almost drowned out the sound of the coach's worn out engine.

After a few hours in Moscow we soon got a taste of life and food behind the Iron Curtain. The food was inedible and boiled in lard. The meat was prehistoric and team members were going down like bowling pins. This one with diarrhoea. This one with stomach upset. The next with both. People told us that the Russian "Mafia" controlled food shipments. If a hotel was not in favour all it got was the worst and oldest provisions. There was no vodka to be had, to our surprise, but...the champagne was fantastic.

All paranoia about black-market dealing became unjustified as time went on. Russians needed hard currency to buy consumer goods and to travel. The state turned an increasingly blind eye to what was happening. For example, we pulled up at the Sport Hotel in a suburb of Moscow late on the second evening. Feeling virtuous, we gave the taxi driver the correct fare, complete with a healthy tip all in roubles. He gave a derisive snort, calculatedly ripped the money into small pieces and burned rubber as he took off into the Moscow night. Roubles have no value on international markets. Needless to say, Russians want only foreign currency so that they may buy consumer goods such as VCRs and TVs. Their enthusiasm for TV seems somewhat misplaced as there is only one awful, mind-numbingly boring channel. Summer reruns of 15-year-old sitcoms look good by comparison.

I have had dealings with supposedly the most difficult taxi drivers in the world—New York, London, Mexico City. Apparently, I had more to learn. A Russian taxi will only pick you up if you're going in his direction. Otherwise, you have to climb in and refuse to get out. I did this the next time but a car slammed into my taxi. My driver, a cynical soul named Michael, jumped out, cursed a few times, and kicked the dent in the side. Meanwhile all the traffic had stopped to let by a large black limousine which was full of politicians. "Gorbachev," Michael said with a sardonic smile and a dismissing wave of the hand, indicating his scorn of the communist hierarchy. Looking back, I wonder if he had any inkling of the momentous events soon to happen.

Because I speak some Russian, I suggested we see the Kremlin and then go shopping. We went to the ZUM, pronounced "Zoom," a version of the GUM, pronounced "Goom" and Moscow's largest department store. Both names are abbreviations of Russian words meaning state-run stores. The place was full of rural people on holiday, busily buying junk. The goods were so shoddy that they would not make even a garage sale in Canada. However, I bought several "Matiushkas." These are the fabled round-cheeked smiling dolls which you open up to find another doll that you open to find yet another...

Shopping in the Soviet Union is a painful, time-consuming business. You ask the price at the counter then go to the cashier to pay. You get a ticket and give it to the sales clerk. You pick up the goods in another line-up. This Russian make-work project takes ages. There is so little worth buying or even available that line-ups form wherever rumour says there is something to buy. Even so since the new reforms, it now costs roughly two weeks' wages to buy a kilo of salami.

The Canadian Embassy gave us a reception to meet the Moscow dignitaries and foreign diplomats as well as some Russian climbers. Then we boarded a bus probably first used by the Czar on imperial picnics. It took us to the airport to fly to Osh in Kyrgyzstan. We dubbed the Soviet official airline Aeroflot "Aeroflop" or "Aeroplop," depending on how critical we felt. Its planes seem always to take off at 3:01 a.m. precisely after making the passengers wait four hours. I thought that Aeroflot personnel may be so ashamed of their lack of security that they feel they have to spirit tourists around at night. On one occasion, I walked on to the runway among at least a hundred planes and rummaged around in two carts before I found my baggage. I could have been planting bombs or cabbages. No one stopped me.

We were not the only mountaineers bound for Osh. Nor were we the only ones worried about Aeroflot security. Every time we stopped over, took off or landed, a group of Finnish mountaineers, also en route to the Pamirs, would wipe their foreheads in terror, shake hands with relief, and pass around paint-remover Soviet cognac. The flight attendant, Olga, svelte but menacing, tried to rule with an iron hand. She had everyone move their baggage from the overhead bins to under the seats. Soon as she disappeared, back went the baggage accompanied by a communal laugh. We reckoned she worked for "Smersh," as in the James Bond film *From Russia with Love.* Thus, we speculated, she must have had a spring-loaded stiletto in the toe of her boot.

Eventually we arrived. We did not on our way to Mount Communism linger long enough to form any opinion of Osh. That would come later. At high speed, our police escort forced carts and chickens from the road. Fourteen dusty, bumpy hours later, the bus arrived at Achik-Tash, the basecamp for Mount Lenin. While here, we visited the chilly graves of the women climbers who had been trapped and killed in a terrible storm on Peak Lenin in 1974. It was very sobering. As we walked solemnly by, we looked at the victims' photographs on the headstones. The leader Elvira Shataeveya was strikingly beautiful. She was also very capable. Their trip was hauntingly awful. Each terrible minute until the last person died was radio-monitored by Vitaly Abalakov, a mountaineering legend in his own right. In 1990, the year after we had visited this camp, forty-two climbers were killed by an ice avalanche. Climbing is not for the unwary. I go climbing on an irregular basis so that the laws of probability will not catch up with me — or so I believe.

We had a mixed bag of food here. The tinned crab from the Bering Sea and the no-name-brand salmon were delectable. However, the caviar and other foods were of little use on the mountain. We had brought lots of instant dinners called Magic Pantries which we immediately renamed "Magic panties." There was no woman among us to protest.

On our second day, we were invited to a celebration hosted by the powers-that-be in Kyrgyzstan and the Soviet Mountaineers Association. The affair left us wide-eyed. The Kyrgyz officials are presumed to be direct descendants of Genghis Khan. All the men kissed each other constantly while the women hung around in the background, wondering—I thought—if they would ever be needed again. Two of the Soviet climbers we met had already climbed Everest. Tough, those Russians. We crawled into the communal yurt, the traditional Mongol tent made from goat's skin, to drink tea and socialise with the teams of many nations. That night, Ernie organised a song contest. While we sampled home-made East German schnapps and the wonderful Russian champagne, we sang the "traditional" Canadian song, *Swing Low Sweet Chariot*, and did a visual rendition of the words. One of the Finnish team was so impressed that he drank too much too fast and passed out. After that, six people used him as a sofa.

All the Russian basecamp tents were the same colour; therefore, many people made it home only after a prolonged, inebriated search. Some never made it at all. An army helicopter, the pronunciation of which sounded to western ears like "gelicopter" took us to Fortambek Camp at the foot of Mt. Communism. It was a spectacular ride over

Training on Mount Communism, 24 500 feet.

rocky ridges, lost canyons and isolated yurt encampments. In contrast to the ruggedness of the highlands, sheep dotted the bucolic lower valleys.

Moulding our organisation into the Russian system took awhile, but eventually we fitted into their acclimatisation schedules: climb high, sleep high. They were in marked contrast to western ideas of climb high, sleep low. Usually in the west we would descend perhaps a thousand feet every night. Nine days after leaving Moscow, some of us were sleeping at 20 000 feet, too abrupt a change for my liking. Groans, avalanches, and vomiting noises alternated in the still of the night.

The climbing was loose, dangerous, and enjoyable only to a dyed-in-the-wool masochist. We depended upon fixed ropes on key areas to speed our progress. As we climbed, we were trying to determine who worked best with whom in order to guarantee the best performance on Everest.

Storms and avalanches at this camp kept sending everyone down, including a friendly Swede. He suffered from cerebral oedema, or water on the brain, which is caused by lack of oxygen. Poor Gustav's head looked like an old soccer ball. Luckily he recovered after descending, the best cure for all altitude problems.

Jana was a woman on the Czech national team who had climbed a hair- raising new route on Peak Leningrad. She burst into tears of frustration when we told her we could save over $1 000 in a month as well as climb wherever we wished. She needed a year's hard work to raise that kind of cash and had to wait for permission to climb even the simplest mountain.

Basecamp was no less dangerous than the upper slopes. One morning Al looked out after what sounded like a howitzer blast to see a mile-wide avalanche heading for the camp. He had a wide but crooked grin. Wide-eyed, he shouted, "Where do you run to?" James ran into a tent, grabbed a camera, and managed to film the event. The commentary is v-v-e-r-r-y s-s-h-h-a-k-y, especially when the avalanche hit the tents. No one was injured; we were only shaken and stirred up.

Eventually after awful weather, acute mountain sickness headaches, pneumonia, and other nasties, the eight of us traversed the twelve kilometres of the world's longest plateau at the height of 20 000 feet and established Camp Three. A crab and cognac party was held to fend off altitude sickness or so we rationalised. Four members went higher to the cold, wind-blown height of 23 000 feet. Part way up, Tim's feet became too constricted in his boots and he had to return.

On this climb I got to know Mario Bilodeau, who was with a Quebec team on Mount Communism. He would eventually join us on the Everest climb. He was involved in a dramatic rescue near the summit of Mount Communism. Mario saved one climber's life but a Czech in another party was not so lucky. He fell in a crevasse, a thin hole a hundred feet deep, and died.

Crazy Myk "Kurt," so-called now because of his antics with a camera on the rooftop of Goom while evading the Moscow police, made the summit but not without mishap. He was close to the summit, very tired, when suddenly a hole opened beneath his feet. Luckily he landed in soft snow fifteen feet down. As this was protected from the wind, he decided to spend the night there. It was relatively warm. The next morning finding himself still alive, he fought his way to the top at 25 000 feet. He was the only one of our team who made the summit, and he was one of only five who made it to the summit out of the two hundred climbers who attempted it that year.

The weather was dangerously bad, and we descended in zero visibility with constant avalanches pouring all around us. Through rotten snow which gave way under our boots, we climbed down into a remote valley where the Russians had another basecamp, called Moskvin. Here we were presented with heaven-sent boiled eggs and a well-earned rest. Every helicopter that arrived we hoped was ours but was not. However, we reached Fortambek a short three days later. Perestroika meant bartering was alive; therefore, we traded most of our fancy western equipment for a ride out a day earlier than we were scheduled.

Once back at the Sport Hotel in Moscow, four of the team dropped like flies from food poisoning. In a dramatic case I grabbed an already-unconscious Ross before he hit the ground. The contaminated food was the lingering farewell gift of Osh Airport. The state of Kyrgyzstan left no other images. Of the fabled silk road and the ideas which were conjured by Marco Polo's writings of Samarkand and Tashkent there was no trace. The conformity and "equality" of over six decades of communism had destroyed the buildings of and links to any earlier culture.

Soon after this we were paying $200 a night in a grimy room in central London. It seems you can't win in the East or West.

We had, however, consolidated the team; we had all been way higher than ever before, and had toughened up in the process. A day later we straggled off the plane horribly jet-lagged. A Japanese tourist stumbled over me, as I kissed the tarmac at Vancouver airport. He looked at me, puzzled, as I pointed—very convincingly I thought—in the direction of Mecca. Another stage was over and Everest was drawing ever closer. ⋀

CHAPTER 6

The Buildup

We returned from Russia as a team, not a perfect one, but one which was probably workable. We all liked each other. By this point we had discovered all kinds of things: what qualities we liked and disliked about each other, and who was compatible in a tent with whom, an important consideration. When confined in a small space with another person, that person's most minor irritations can drive you to awful thoughts. For instance, Mike Sullivan, who is a great guy, has a tiny, constant cough—"ahuh, ahuh." A thousand of these and I am ready to kill.

I tend to anaesthetise people with my flatulence; no one is conscious enough to have any feelings at all. However, my snoring is a different matter altogether. On climbs, I have often woken up with a looming shadow over my head. In the half light I have seen a climber with an evil grin and an ice-axe ready to strike, poised for the *coup de grace*. With a blood curdling cry he strikes. Meantime with cat-like agility, I roll out of the way, engulf him in my sleeping bag, thus disarming him. I live to snore another day or night in the malodorous depths of my bag.

Everest was that much closer. It was only months away, as it was now late 1990. We had done our major high altitude acclimatising. We had learned the limits of our compatibility. Yet problems remained. I still had to spend four to six hours on the phone each night to deal with all the arrangements, sponsors and logistics. I also had a full time "day" job. I would be exhausted but sometimes content at 11:00 p.m., when everything had gone well. More often than not, though, there was an unresolved problem: would we get these tents, skis, ropes donated or not? Would a sponsor stop dithering and give us a final yes or no? The logistics became a nightmare and the phone bills for the team crept up to $3 000 per month. We were calling all over the world.

One of the biggest logistics problems was our supplies. Most had to be ordered at least six months in advance, collected in Vancouver, and then shipped off to Nepal to await our arrival. The oxygen cylinders had to be manufactured and the complete systems we needed manufactured in England and then assembled in California. Then they came to Vancouver to be shipped to Nepal. The propane stoves came from Germany and when they arrived in Vancouver, Al was told that we would have to obtain permission from every country over which they flew on their way to Nepal.

The curtain was rising on a bureaucratic show of nightmarish proportions. Al pleaded our cause eloquently and I could just imagine him beating his fists on the ground and then kissing airport employees' feet in rapid succession. Suddenly, because we were climbing for charity, all was magically spirited to Nepal with no problem at all. One problem remained though; the generators which were used for powering the radio system and for lights were very heavy and had to be fine-tuned for altitude. There was no one at the other end to do that. It would have to wait for our arrival.

Funding remained a problem. The second charity ball only just paid for itself, even after months of effort by Peggy Delaney and her committee in Toronto to sell corporate tables and obtain products for a silent auction in which people put in written bids for the goods on display. Peggy is well known in eastern Canada for her tireless work in raising funds for the victims of Rett Syndrome. The continuing recession in eastern Canada made money hard to come by. Charities had to have gimmicks and/or famous actors to attract a crowd. Apparently Everest wasn't enough.

This was the doldrums for us. One by one, potential sponsors dropped out. We discovered, however, the public spirit of Cathay Pacific Airways as well as their need for a great public relations campaign. Then, when we finally had everything in place the Gulf War hit, and people stopped flying. We held our breath lest Cathay Pacific

Airways bailed out. Much to our relief, they didn't. With that, the tide began to turn.

A film company approached me with the idea of doing a documentary on the undertaking. Yaletown Productions, run by Michael Collier of Vancouver, is an often-time award-winning film company. Yaletown applied for help from various corporations to film our adventure. In true cliff-hanging sequence, it was not until a short four weeks before we left that the company received a grant from Canadian Television. If this grant had not happened, the house of cards that was the Everest expedition would have started collapsing, as sponsors needed the exposure that a nationally shown film would generate. Yaletown was essential to us but we were too strapped to underwrite the company. Yet it was in the same position as us—no money.

Moving communication equipment around the world became a bigger problem than we anticipated. Satellite systems are run by monopolies, notably "Telecom" and "Inmarsat," both of which had been preempted by the buildup to the Gulf War. Consequently, Alan Hobson, in Calgary, could obtain no commitment to procure a satellite. We needed one, firstly for rescue purposes, secondly for family communications, and thirdly to advertise ourselves and major sponsors to the world. Imagine the impact of the statement: "This is Cathay Pacific Basecamp on Mount Everest. The team has today reached the North Col." Initially, the Chinese wanted $300 000 US for the privilege of using a satellite dish on Everest. When we said we were not officially "broadcasting," they dropped the fee to a much more reasonable $300 US.

I wrote to many people connected with Everest and the levels of advice given were very different. The famous British climber and expedition organiser, Chris Bonington, said that as every expedition was different, he felt he could not offer any useful advice. Arne Naess, a legendary Norwegian mountaineer, had organised the successful Norwegian climb of Everest some years ago. This team had fantastic weather and put all the members of their team on the top. He offered sound advice to get twelve climbers on the summit: "get more than enough materials as high as possible. Have six climbers alternate breaking trail as often as possible." Reinhold Messner, from Italy, one of the greatest and most visionary climbers of all time, was very supportive but was off to climb the "last great problem in the Himalayas" the South face of Lhotse, a sister peak of Everest. Therefore, he was somewhat preoccupied. Laurie Skreslet was the first Canadian to climb Everest in 1982. His somewhat cynical forecast of what we could expect of sponsors depressed us for several days. With the exception of the few who remained with us, he proved to be too right.

Everything had been taken care of, or so we thought. The food had been packaged during a four-day marathon session by ten climbers and our friends in Clearwater, B.C. It was then trucked to Vancouver and shipped to Nepal. Stoves, ropes, oxygen, tents, personal equipment had gone on ahead and, we hoped, would be waiting for us when we arrived months later.

There were so many loose ends so close to departure time. Despite the problems of transporting the beastly but necessary satellite, Alan had to be in New York on a training course to find out how to use the satellite dish. The visas had come, no they hadn't, despite our sending the Chinese close to $100 000. We had been waiting months for their arrival.

Marge Helminck had been our loyal and dedicated secretary in Prince George. She believed in our venture, and her inspired work, all done voluntarily, was fantastic. Although she had moved to Vancouver, the team wanted her to accompany us to Tibet, much to her surprise and joy. However, to everything there is a cost. Therefore, I put her in charge of the visas. She was very efficient but she worried that the staff in the Chinese Embassy would not give her the visas. They had, she said, a phenomenally advanced form of bureaucracy that probably the rest of the world would have to wait 2 000 years to emulate.

Always one step ahead of Marge, they could spot names in wrong order, a letter missing from a name, occupation not quite right, eye colour not exactly correct. "Oops, three people travelling on a different day must have a group visa. Apply again. It will take only two weeks to process. The processing fee for Canadians is $16 but for Americans only $8.00.

"Why?"

"There is no one here to explain. We close at three today; come back Wednesday as Tuesday is a Chinese holiday."

Aaaaghh! Attack! Kill! Give me a mountain to climb! I couldn't deal with it. Some details such as visas were never totally resolved in spite of months of work. I think it took six months for them to come through. The visa for Myk Kurth to enter Tibet did not materialise until he went personally in conventional western clothing but with long hair hidden, and a fixed and ingratiating grin, to the Chinese Embassy in Kathmandhu. By this time the rest of us had already left Kathmandhu, and Myk had to catch up.

During the week before we left Canada, James and I worked every night until 4:00 a.m. There were up to fifty faxes a day from and to half a dozen countries. The plan was that climbers, spouses, and friends would travel together as far as Everest Basecamp where we would remain together for two weeks. We left Vancouver at different times, planning to rendezvous in Nepal. When James and I said our tearful goodbyes to remaining at-home friends as we departed on the most exciting trip of our lives, we did not know if we would actually return. We were numb with mental exhaustion, not really aware we were finally on our way. ⋀

CHAPTER 7

To the East

C athay Pacific Airways had arranged a large press conference for us at the Pan Pacific Hotel in Vancouver at which Alan Hobson explained the satellite system to the twenty-five representatives of television, radio and newspapers. Ernie gave a moving speech about the Rett Syndrome and what the climb hoped to achieve:

"Ladies and Gentlemen, Peter and the team wish, through this climb of Everest to raise national awareness and one million dollars for the Rett Syndrome to find a cure. I went through the pain and ignorance of uncertainty of watching Sarah, my daughter, slowly deteriorate, from the age of two on, into profound mental disability.

At this time I had no idea what was wrong with her. There are many people in Canada and throughout the world who are like I was eight years ago, and they agonise about their mentally handicapped daughters and have no idea what is really wrong with them. Let me say, help is on the way."

After more than a dozen interviews in Canada, we flew to Hong Kong and to another reception organised by the Hong Kong Businessmen's Association. I expressed my thanks to the chairman and made him aware that the Canada China Friendship Society had facilitated our permit to climb Everest. We were gratified, I said, to see a continuation of this support in Hong Kong.

To promote the expedition, we were invited to climb up the outside of the Canadian International School and so Tim and Alan did just that, in 35°C weather. As the drainpipe they used to fix the protection rope to was loose and rusty, they had to be extremely careful. No one in the audience of one hundred was aware of the problem, but if they fell, the concrete underneath would have been unforgiving. They were good actors. No one outside a few team members guessed their difficulties. When they reached the Canadian flag at the top, festooned with ropes, they hugged each other in triumph. I christened the picture I took of this epic "Gay Boys in Bondage."

On our way to the icefields of Everest was Bangkok, Thailand. It was hot, incredibly polluted and bewildering. We learned the Thai greeting "Sawadee" very quickly and the more forward ones on the team repeated it constantly to the locals, especially to the women who, we all agreed, were the most beautiful women any of us had ever seen. In contrast to the rest of us, Alan Hobson was strangely quiet and somewhat stressed. No wonder. The satellite dish, which had cost him many years of savings, was lost somewhere in Asia. He spent his time waiting by the fax machine in the hotel.

Wayne Beebe, a friend from Prince George had come along as support to look after friends and relations going to basecamp. Mario, James, Alan, John, Wayne and I ventured downtown to see the most notorious red light district in the world, Patpong. We entered a bar. When John was propositioned, he bent his wrist in a saucy way and said in a high-pitched voice with a knowing smile, "Sorry, dear, I'm with him," referring to Alan. Alan was more surprised than the woman who vanished in short order.

Wayne was propositioned also. In his haste to avoid a scene, he gave the woman $20 US which he mistook for twenty Thai bhat, worth about $1. I said to him, "That was very generous of you to subsidise the local economy."

The management of the bar presented me with a bill for $100 and locked us in when we refused to pay. Adrenaline flowed; I grabbed the goon by the door. He, by the way, weighed at least 250 pounds and stood six foot five, an unusual size in Asia. I lifted him out of the way and moved the bolt on the door. We hightailed it into the street before the staff regrouped. I was starting to feel like Humphrey Bogart in the *Maltese Falcon.*

The next bit of excitement was not long in coming. Crossing a street shortly after this, Mario failed to see a motorcycle bearing down on him at high speed. The driver, Mario, and the vehicle went down in a blur of legs and machinery. We rushed up. "Mario, are you hurt?" He wasn't moving and I could see one leg twisted at right angles to where it should be.

"Bang goes his chances at Everest," I thought. He stood up and shook himself. I thought "Wow, these Quebequois are really tough. No wonder they want to separate. They think we're all wimps."

Mario was fine. He was also uninjured. It was the driver's leg I had seen in the dark. The team began to relax after all the stressful events of the previous weeks as we saw the sights of Bangkok. These included emerald Buddhas, golden Buddhas, floating markets, and even a huge python that wound itself round everyone except me who moved out of the way at twenty-five miles per hour.

At a Thai festival we saw mystical dancing and cockfights. There were elephants giving rides, and I have never seen Timo run as fast as he did when a four-ton one answered a call of nature right beside him. The Finnish word for "help" is really strange.

Thailand is wonderful. Despite our experience in the bar, we found it non-threatening. I think we felt this way because Thais are devout Buddhists who abhor violence. While the men do two years compulsory military service, this is balanced somewhat by the three months many of them spend in monasteries afterward.

We visited the bridge over the River Kwai. It was part of a railway to carry Japanese supplies to Burma during the Second World War. The Japanese had built it using prisoner-of-war labour. The bridge is immortalised in the memories of people over the age of forty and movie buffs of any age by the film *Bridge Over the River Kwai* starring Alec Guinness. I strained hard to hear the echoes of *Colonel Bogey March* as whistled by the prisoners of war in the movie.

There was crisis after crisis in moving our tons of equipment and selves from Canada to Bangkok; unknown rules, excess baggage costs, faxes everywhere, continuing uncertainty. The more the Buddhist outlook absorbed me, the less the crises mattered. It would all work out.

Our next phase of travel would land us in Nepal. This was the beginning of the real thing. On the route, we flew close by Everest and the team went quiet as everyone contemplated the forbidding mountain. Tim, who usually does not drink, was into the Bailey's Irish Cream, compliments of the Royal Nepal Airlines. He was merry as a mediaeval lord.

Once we arrived, hordes of porters insisted on carrying our gear to the waiting minibuses in Kathmandhu and we arrived at the Potala Palace Hotel, in the district of Thamel. What a zoo! Kathmandhu has been called a "Venerable Enigma," but this really meant nothing until I arrived there.

The culture shock stuns even the experienced traveller. While Nepal lacks the violence of many third-world countries, it has its own nastiness. While there are splendid hotels costing $200 a night, our hotel by contrast, was clean and cost $3 a night. There are beggars with no legs. The largest open sewer system in the world sprawls here. People barely subsist day to day. We in the West have no understanding of this until we see the appalling awfulness of third world poverty. Despite it all, the people are incredibly cheerful and friendly. In Kathmandhu, even in the face of the onrushing tide of mass tourism, few are gouging. In Mexico, even Thailand, we were seen as "foreign marks." Not in Kathmandhu. We lost ourselves and our sense of direction in the clamour and bustle of the narrow streets, as we avoided ancient, decrepit taxis and the ever-present venerated cows. I went into a hospital created by Mother Theresa and saw people in the last stages of every disease I have ever heard about. A Hindu Sadhu, or holy man, wearing only a dirty white loincloth, lifted a rock with what we presumed was his penis. We saw a cremated body down by the river; only a foot remained.

Monkeys swarmed everywhere, but apparently only at a particular time of day: 2:00 p.m. As I wore glasses I didn't get too close because the monkeys would rip them off me. Sensing how overwhelmed some of our companions were by the culture shock, I promised to organise an expedition to British Columbia Parliament Buildings in Victoria the next year so that we could compare monkeys.

The Nepalese establishment, like the Indian one, emulates British customs where the powers-that-be are more British than the British still stuck in the time-warp of the last days of the Empire. Tea, crumpets, and cricket are still available in many lingering corners of the world and Kathmandhu is one of these. It would make a perfect setting for a Somerset Maugham novel.

Marge, Wayne and I cycled into the mountains to visit an ancient town called Niktipur. We called out "meep, meep", road-runner style, to make people know we were coming. They all smiled and loved this total silliness. Our visit had a purpose. In the 18th century, the local males of Niktipur had rebelled against the ruler and he had cut all their ears and noses off. The grisly weapons, long knives, were still on display in the village square.

I discovered, back in Kathmandhu, that all our boxes of food which had been in storage for two months had been kept outside at the airport. The monsoon rains had nearly ruined them. We patched them up as best we could and then waited in the customs lineup to pay the customs fees. All attempts at bribery, a way of life in the East, failed, and we had to pay in rupees. I handed over an inch of Canadian dollars and received fourteen inches of notes in exchange. Jamie climbed on the counter in the customs office to film me handing it over. The customs men saw the funny side, so we got through with no more hassle, although we did have to pay.

Jamie Clarke supervises unpacking of supplies at Kathmandu.

Ashley Ford, a journalist from the *Vancouver Province*, had been commissioned by Cathay Pacific to file reports back to them on the progress of the expedition. He spoke fluent Chinese; later on the expedition he would try to school us in the right ways of dealing with our liaison officer, Mr. Li. "Ni hao, tongjer" meant "good day, comrade," but the effort required to say "tongjer" was really something. The "jer " sound started in the stomach and worked its way up to the larynx, to emerge like the last stages of whooping cough. Chinese is a weird language indeed. Ashley, Marge, several others and I took off for the mountain villages in a battered taxi. I had a Nepalese phrase book and was sitting right behind the driver so he could not see me. I jabbered away in Nepalese. He was totally fooled and when I exclaimed "Rakshi! Baagh!" (Stop, tiger!) he almost swerved off the road. Then he realised there are no tigers in this part of Nepal and we all had a good laugh.

There were thirty-five of us at this point. Ashley was watching our personalities and interactions very carefully. I find it fascinating that, as I got to know people, the image I have of their personalities changes constantly until it finally crystallises at a particular point and that is the image that stays with me. My impression of Ashley crystallised around this time.

His computer crashed and so, to pass the time creatively, he made up a Harlequin-style romance story about climbers. The climbers were heavily involved in various types of international intrigue, using climbing mount Everest as a front while vying for the hand of the ravishingly-beautiful Nastasya, a Russian emerald smuggler in Kathmandhu. He had us in fits one night in a restaurant as everyone sat around cross legged on raised seats, like eastern potentates.

Here's the story, greatly embellished by myself. Any resemblance to people living or dead is purely fictitious or intentional. Sven, the rugged blond ice-cold Swede, is in cold storage and watching closely the antics of Raphael, the unscrupulous, urbane and meaningfully pony-tailed Canadian, who, unknown to Nastasya, murdered her previous husband by slipping an undetectable poison into his breakfast egg. Posing as Errol Flynn's twin brother, he uses his dashing charm to convince her of untold wealth lying unseen for centuries in a cave in Tibet, close to Mount Everest. Psychotic Max, from Catnip, Saskatchewan, has eavesdropped and hopes to eliminate Raphael and Nastasya to make off with the jewels. The culture shock of Nepal is making him doubt reality even more than usual. He is suffering from paranoid schizophrenic gastrointestinal cramps every twenty seconds and hence is very indecisive. Dark and mysterious Maurice, from west of the Rio St. Lawrence, would love to get in on the act because he has information on the whereabouts of the cave. Unfortunately his visa from Tibet has not shown up yet, and he has also run out of luck. The hulking bear-like-but-cuddlesome Henri from Suqueegie, Quebec, has been following Raphael for five years to avenge himself of the loss of his mistress, Jaime Les Hommes. Meanwhile, the indomitable and gaunt Inspector Clousieau is slowly closing in, waiting until the jewels are found, and collecting evidence to nab everybody, to advance his career to the justice department in the highest ranks of the redoubtable SRPPM. (Society for the Re-institution of Pink Panther Movies.)

The plot thickens as we are informed by Mountain Travel in Kathmandhu that our Sherpas will arrive tomorrow and that our buses and trucks to take us to the Tibet border will arrive shortly.

We met our Sherpas in Kathmandhu. Ang Nima, the Sirdar, or leader of the four other Sherpas, is a benign and very wise person for his thirty-eight years. He has an oval face so I called him "Oval nima." As I was the leader, he thought I would be always very serious and very straightforward. When I would say something like, "Ang, We have no more money; you have to go home," he would look astonished before realizing I was only joking. His teeth would then flash in a huge grin.

Lhakpa had already climbed Everest with Pat Morrow in 1982 and was phenomenally strong. I saw him carry a 300-pound case for a mile up a 45-degree slope. He has legs like cedar trunks. We gave him some money to buy supplies, but because Nepalese are not allowed to possess foreign currency, he was arrested, beaten and thrown in jail. What a way to treat your national heroes! James, Al and I went to the law courts to plead for him but the judges, with menacing smiles said, "If you keep arguing, we'll put you in jail instead of Lhakpa." James started to argue but Al and I grabbed one arm each side and frog-marched him out, while maintaining obsequious smiles. Nepalese jails are the ultimate degradation: five cents a day for food and all the rats you can play with.

Ang Tsering, the cook, was so eager to please, he would patiently cook anything you wanted whenever you wanted it. Sometimes the requests were repeated orders of French fries, which were to taste great up at Basecamp. Because of his desire to please, I called him "Answering Service."

Dawa was keen on noodles after midnight so he was called "Dawa Noodle." Our fifth Sherpa Ang Temba ate so many Japanese-type "Ichiban" food he was called "Itchy Temba."

The Sherpas were Buddhist, very serene, totally unflappable and philosophical. "You'll die anyway and return as something else, so don't worry" seemed to symbolise their approach to life. They had a handle on our western-style crises. For instance when we were trying to get to the border and were held up for a week, they said, "Today this has much importance. There are also many other things in the world important to many other people. Tomorrow it will not be so important. Life is like this."

The Sherpas have been brought into the 20th century by tourism and other travellers to the mountains. It is therefore ironic that they do not regard the mountains as beautiful scenery as we do. They never comment on the landscape that they hold sacred, but strangely do not see as beautiful. Unfortunately, their culture is disappearing. For example, Sherpa children, born in or near Kathmandhu, may speak Nepalese when addressed by their parents in Sherpa. They may even become embarrassed if they have to speak Sherpa.

I asked our guides how other expeditions had treated them. On the whole, they were happy. Sherpas are the new elite of Nepal. The money they make on one expedition is much more than most of the population earn in a year, a sum which is about $600. The Sherpas receive new clothing from each expedition they guide. This factor alone can bring their yearly income up to ten times the average person's income.

While buying the rest of the needed supplies, we continued to have a good time in the city with these fascinating, accommodating Nepalese. Late one night, Mike, James and I hired several rickshaws and tickled the drivers so they couldn't drive properly. Installing them in the passenger seats, we raced through Kathmandhu, pedalling furiously, scattering chickens, dogs and other creatures to the four winds. Wonderful training for Everest while the monsoon rains pelted down! We had Nepalese dragons emblazoned on our expedition jackets to symbolise protection. We borrowed this idea from the dragons who guard the king's palace.

Finally we had to leave. Because trucks may only enter the inner city of Kathmandhu in the early morning when these narrowest streets in the world are empty, we were up at 4:00 a.m. Our two trucks were waiting for us, together with our buses in the street outside the hotel. I woke up to the sound of numerous men clearing their throats and spitting on the street, a common occurrence every morning, but nauseating to the outsider.

The film crew filmed our noisy departure, and we settled down for the wild ride to the border. The buses wound their way through terraced fields of maize. The Himalayas glinted distantly in the monsoon murk, giving us tantalising glimpses of their hidden delights, or was it horrors? We passed many smiling barefooted people and occa-

Nepal monsoon.

sionally a clerk or businessman, clad in a strangely comical outfit of tight pants, business jacket, and hat that was similar to the World War II British army hat which is shaped like a tiny upturned canoe.

The bus lurched and slid across the road. We rushed to the window to gaze down on an ocean of mud that lapped at the wheel tops. Mexico's goop was nothing compared to this. We were stuck. Everyone helped to lay all the stones we could find under and in front of the wheels. We slithered uneasily onwards. The drop to the gorge bottom grew ever deeper. We were glad to be on the right hand side of the road, away from the clutches of the swollen Sun Kosi River thundering its way to the plains of India. Round the next bend a few buses were stopped. Several of us got off the bus and ran up to the stopped buses. We discovered the reason they were stopped: a mountain was falling on the road. Rocks as big as Volkswagen Beetles were dropping from thousands of feet above. The blockage, a hundred yards wide, had wrecked the road. Meanwhile the rain did not let up. Mist swirled around and gave the whole scene an air of unreality. Unbelievably, this was the main highway to Tibet.

Our only option was to return to Kathmandhu while our equipment stayed at the landslide in the forlorn hope it could get through. Because the customs had sealed it with a lead seal, there was no way we could break the seal. But we needed some of it for immediate use. Ross and I spent the next two days in a bureaucratic maze to obtain permission to break the seal and pull out what we needed. Finally we waited for two hours in a humid office near the royal palace while the head of customs languidly perused and finally granted our humble request. The office fan turned very slowly.

It was another crisis but adopting the prevailing attitude of the country, I said to myself, "We're doing all we can. Relax. Worse things happen at sea."

The director of the film team wanted us to bribe the Nepalese bulldozer driver who was waiting at the landslide for the rain and bombardment to cease. With a bribe, the director argued, the driver would immediately clear the road. But because the bulldozer had merely a canvas roof, I felt he would be exposed to needless risk. I understood that the film team had a limited time period, and the director had to get back to Kathmandhu for other engagements. But this was the East.

The team was becoming anxious and a "State of the Union" address became necessary. I wanted to reaffirm my leadership philosophy so I said:

"I just want to make you all aware that my whole leadership thrust so far has been for us to work together and look after delegated jobs. The whole team has worked miracles so far in every way. The best guy for the job has that job, with some degree of consultation. I only reserve the right to make the final decision. This is not a 'follow the leader' type of scenario so be aware that we have a group process. A leader has to interpret the wishes of the group but can veto any action at any time. I will not do this, preferring to take a spectator's viewpoint, overseeing the operation. We're doing great up to this point and with patience we'll get through. You do not shout and scream and make authoritarian decisions in the East. You lay back and wait for events to happen, molding them where and if you can."

I had picked my climbing team and they understood my approach. They were not hired hands to be ordered around but committed professionals working equally.

The film crew didn't see things from the same perspective. They wanted me to play "Boss" and do something. Fortunately, a talk with Mike Collier, the producer of the film crew straightened this out. Mike is a fun-loving, understanding guy for whom I have much respect. I told him that we westerners are all goal-oriented, striving to get somewhere in the shortest possible path. Life doesn't necessarily support this view. If we let these obstacles we had to face bother us, we'd go nuts. It all works out. The western self esteem depends on gaining approval of other people for the things we do. When we fail in reaching a goal, we feel the failure is a personality fault and our self esteem drops. Also in the present circumstances, I could picture the international incident if I had railroaded the Nepalese and the driver had been killed.

Four days later the road was cleared, and our trucks got through, only to be stopped by more landslides five miles from the border. John, Dennis, and Mario went ahead with the Sherpas to round up four hundred local porters, at a cost of $2 000, to move the gear around the slides.

The day's entry in my diary says "Twenty-five hill tribesmen ambushed Dennis and ran off with all the Red River cereal. Thank God."

Arriving at this set of slides, we discovered yet another landslide bigger than the first. After I had made the decision to keep going, we established a series of lookouts at points along the slide. Time had run out; the Chinese trucks had already been waiting for a week with the meter ticking on inexorably. I, like everyone else, knew the extreme danger we were in, but rationalised we were here partly for danger anyway. What was a little more?

Dennis volunteered to be our shepherd; the thirty of us, in pairs, as well as the ten local Nepalese, made a run for it. Boulders crashed down within two feet of us while we headed for the only shelter to be had—under a small overhanging piece of rock—before venturing out

The big landslide.

into the boulder firing line again. I imagined the Battle of the Somme, in the first world war. I am used to mountaineering hazards but this was terrifyingly different. I had a similar feeling of dread and apprehension when I was canoeing up the Inside Passage between Vancouver Island and the British Columbia Mainland. Then three, twenty-five foot-long killer whales surfaced right by my canoe and I thought for one terrifying minute that I was whale bait.

The mud was up to our knees and "running" was very slow. It was like the dream where the grizzly bear is after you and your feet are weighed down like lead. "Splat." A boulder landed. Hit, Dennis went down in the mud, picked himself up, and made it to the far side. He had been only grazed but it was close. Tim cleaned him off in the next stream and we marched on to the border, which was about twelve miles away. Tragically a French woman was killed at the same place the following day. ⋀

"I survived the mudslide – an
adventure in itself."

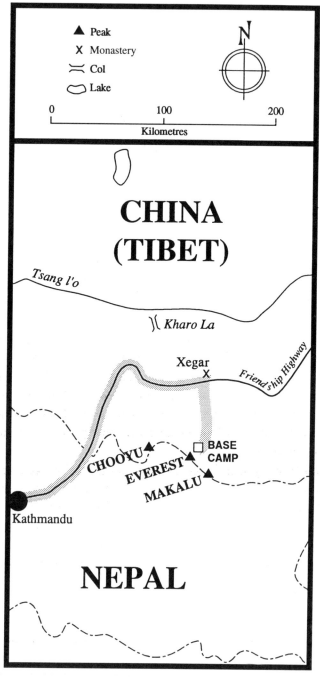

Route from Kathmandu to Everest.

CHAPTER 8

In Tibet

T he Chinese liaison officer Mr. Li and the interpreter Louis were waiting for us at the border at Zhangmu. They informed us that we would owe them another $2 000 because the trucks had waited the extra week. The "I Ching" is a famous Chinese philosophical work but the name resembles the sound of a cash register. We therefore formally christened the CMA or Chinese Mountaineering Association "I Ching" because of its money-grabbing habits.

We were too honest with the customs, which Louis called "customers." Our food was costed out in Canadian dollars. We realized the mistake of this but lacked time to change it. It cost us a stinging $3 000. The team had to dole out more money and this was becoming the proverbial pain in the ass.

Our first night in Tibet was spent at a hotel in Nyalam, just over the border. The hotel was a barracks and a mess but the food in the neighbouring restaurant was wonderful. It was the last time in Tibetan restaurants we would have more than awful-tasting, subsistence-size rations. We were charged a mandatory $68 US per night per person in the hotels for cold, draughty rooms with non-functioning toilets. We had to use the communal latrine next to the restaurant. We suffered smells that would make even Genghis Khan dream of new worlds and cleaner latrines to conquer. But with fortitude and lack of alternatives, we straddled the holes in the floor and prayed we wouldn't miss.

The next morning saw a huge tide of Tibetan porters surging back and forth outside the hotel. In contrast to the passive, Buddhist attitudes we had grown to love, these porters were anxious to get their hands on our stuff to carry it up the steep hillside. After handing over another bundle of local currency, we were off, keeping a close eye on the porters. We did not want the gear to be spirited into the many waiting households on the way up to the mountainside.

All the way up through the wet jungle there were exotic flowers and birds. Marijuana plants grew everywhere. Leeches somehow got into our boots. Huge boulders had dropped in the rain and were poised just above our heads about to continue downward, taking anything and everything with them.

The next stage in the odyssey was the most spectacular road any of us had ever been on: twelve miles of a twisting, fifteen-foot wide horror with a drop of 1 500 feet straight down to the raging waters below. The chain-smoking, surly truck drivers careened round the bends at breakneck speed while massive, cascading waterfalls fell from thousands of feet above, to pass over our heads that were protected by only the occasional wooden deflector above the road. Louis said, "never any accidents." But under one bridge, reposing gracefully in the river, was an ant-like rusting bus. I craned my neck for skeletons. The lump in my throat was growing menacingly.

We reached another, even bigger barracks of a hotel. The floors were wet from the dripping ceilings. As we were going to our austere monks' cells, a huge black pig ran by and vanished through a broken window. Al uttered a haunting and visceral hunting cry similar to the ones first voiced by his ancestors in the forests of old Germany. He gave chase but the wily pig was too quick for him. "Damn," he said, "we could've roasted that in the main foyer tonight and had something decent to eat for a change."

We found out that night that a Belgian expedition had got away with only $28 in custom duties. Live and learn. That night John and Mario discovered that the so-called hot water system in the hotel was on "meltdown" and had started a small fire which Mario noticed in the nick of time. Why he bothered, I don't know; the hotel needed demolishing anyway. We didn't mind the ancient warehouses of hotels so much as the exorbitant rates the CMA charged. Who received the money? Probably, the higher up in the Communist party the dignitary was, the more money he got. I had noticed in Russia that the system there was more capitalistic than the West in this respect.

We suddenly emerged on to the high Tibetan Plateau at 12 000 feet. It was gratifyingly drier but much more barren. Stopping at a village, I wandered through to find the legendary Tibetan prophet Milarepa's tomb. A child sidled up to me and I was startled to see five holes in his face where his features should have been. It was leprosy, I think.

We drove through a wild and open landscape on dirt roads for six hours and came to the top of a mountain pass at 16 500 feet. Reaching this height so quickly is not advisable. It makes a person feel as if drugged on demerol. You can't breathe, a condition causing panic if you don't watch out.

Arriving in Tingri, a small Tibetan town, some of the team watched the slaughter of a goat. The villagers pulled the stomach out first and then killed the animal from the inside. I don't think they realise that animals can feel pain or maybe they just do not care.

Chomolungma is the Tibetan word for Everest and means "Mother Goddess of the World." That being so, we expected a bit more of The Chomolungma Hotel but it was another barracks and even

Tibetan farmer.

more disorganised than the last. While visas for Tibet are hard to come by, they allow you to stay in this hotel for more a reasonable price of $3 instead of the standard $68.

As I passed James in the hallway he said, "Guess what I saw just now."

"Go on."

"A female hotel employee ducked under the stairwell over there, threw up, wiped her mouth, and carried on. Yuck."

This did not bide well for the food; and, in fact, the menu consisted of rubber bread, old peanuts, ancient pickled cabbage from the time of the Opium Wars, chopped up animal of some sort, and peas barely recognisable as peas. The beer was good, though.

The mountains around had soft, springy turf and were a joy to hike on. These were important conditions for acclimatisation. A local woman, bronzed and wizened, offered us "tsampa," a dish made from barley. All the local people had to eat apart from this dish was goat meat, yak meat, and a few vegetables.

Xegar Dzong, a famous 12th century monastery that was vandalised by Chinese forces in 1950 still housed friendly monks and we

Tibetan nomads.

decided to visit. We had been warned about rabid dogs at the site, and so went armed with ski poles to fight off the attacking hordes. Not a single dog showed up, but the nettles we had to walk through to reach the fortress above the monastery were vicious.

As we climbed, the monks started chanting an incessant refrain that drifted eerily up among the ancient fortifications on the hillside. Tibetan monks have an inveterate sense of humour, so they happily tried on our hats and sunglasses, and giggled at the effect.

I was out walking on the second day about five miles away from the village in a remote valley and noticed a black, upright creature too tall for a bear high up on a ridge about a mile away. Intrigued I followed it, but I never got within half a mile of it. I regretted not having time to investigate.

Mr. Li negotiated with the truck drivers who have much power as they control transport. We selected four trucks and one jeep to get us through the sodden highland to Everest Basecamp. The monsoon still affected this area although not as badly as in Nepal. Two sleepy checkpoints later, we were on a steeply sloping, wet road that threatened to roll away into the fog below. The first glimpse of Everest was stimulating and awe-inspiring. It was almost a religious experience as we all felt its attraction. To show the depth of his feelings, Tim did a headstand while facing Everest.

The trucks battled swollen streams as we fought our way to the Rongbuk Monastery some four miles from Everest Basecamp. We were invited by the head Lama to a reception where we were given tea with salt and rancid butter. When we finished a glass, it was immediately refilled so we sipped it very slowly. We were afraid that to not drink the tea would give offence. We were feeling our way very carefully in this weird, mediaeval country which hasn't changed for thousands of years.

The Rongbuk Monastery, at close to 17 000 feet, is apparently the highest permanently inhabited settlement on earth. I wondered how the monks could exist here with such depleted oxygen levels. A person can get used to anything, I guess. Part of the walls of the buildings inside the courtyard had been rebuilt with old expedition hut walls, giving a strangely European flavour to the surroundings. There was a German name "Max Eiselin, Muenchen" on the wall beside me as I sat slowly sipping my rancid yak-buttered tea. It was an interesting juxtaposition.

We drank the tea with six bald Tibetans in greasy, armless red robes while the heavy, wet monsoon snow wafted down outside, filling every crevice. There was no heating, but the monks didn't seem to feel the cold. Their expressions were never less than spiritual and welcoming. When some monks started a haunting chant inside the monastery, I suffered a strange feeling of *deja vu*. It was the return of the feeling of total cultural shock that I had had first experienced on a trip alone to Italy when I was sixteen. A sense of unreality persisted, then and at the monastery.

Al said, "Come, and look at this." Inside the gloomy, juniper scented building was a decaying, gold-leaf-covered altar full of old relics and vessels. Among these artifacts were numerous pictures of the Dalai Lama, in various poses but he was always smiling. A picture of him is a most treasured gift in Tibet, and I had brought many copies of a photograph of him with me. Tibetans are always asking for pictures of him, but his pictures are forbidden by the Chinese. If I were caught with a photo, I could have been charged with sedition

Rongbuk Monastery.

and thrown out of the country—or worse.

Visions of lying on a concrete floor, arms outstretched and a drop of water dripping every two seconds on my forehead for an unspecified period— the tourist image of the Chinese water torture— made me very careful when giving out any of my photocopies.

I was dying to ask for a demonstration of the famed levitation powers the monks are supposed to have, but restrained myself. By chance, my curiosity would be satisfied on our final day here. The image of this monastery that remains with me is a monk standing motionless on a rock, legs spread out, robe thrown around his neck and blowing in the wind, face pointing upward to heaven. As we drove off into the blizzard, the snow increased in intensity, swirled and partly obscured him as I looked back. I am almost certain he lifted into the air as he vanished into the gloomy, wet snow.

The truck I was in keeled over thirty degrees. We all piled out. The road at this point ran alongside the Rongbuk River, which had washed the road away. The Sherpas and the Chinese drivers worked together to pile up stones and we rumbled on to the desolate, windswept, and wildly beautiful Basecamp site.

The spot where Mallory had camped in 1924 was vacant, so we pitched our thirty tents on the only piece of grass for miles around. It was obvious from the old photos of 1924 that nothing had changed. The boulders and landscape were identical to photos of Mallory's camp.

I couldn't believe the amount of migrant birds there. There were flocks of pigeons; marauding bands of alpine choughs, a kind of crow with bright red beak; pied wagtails bobbing everywhere; fat bullfinches; and even a few sandpipers. A lammergeier or alpine kite, a huge buzzard, wheeled overhead, giving its pathetic, tinny cat-like cry which was most out of keeping for a bird of its size and majesty.

We even had a stream running through the camp. Everest towered above at the far end of the valley. Peaks and glaciers sparkled all round. High up on the ridge above the camp was an inaccessible black rock formation, identical to an Easter Island statue. Maybe Thor Heyerdahl can trace the origins of the Easter Island people back to Tibet.

Our large Basecamp "Habitat" tent, on loan from Design Shelter Systems, was fabulously stable and quiet in the wind. Nearby, the

Indian expedition's tent cracked constantly with sounds like pistol shots. Ernie, who suffered more serious headaches than any of us did at 17 200 feet, went to Lhasa and then back to Toronto, leaving us at the mercy of Everest for the next two months. We put up our tents in a raging snowstorm. It had taken a month of effort just to get here from Canada.

My site was on Mallory's. I could feel his presence.

No one did much for three days. Altitude headaches came and went. I sneaked in on James one morning and took a picture as he woke up. His face was still a wizened ruin but slowly improving.

He noticed me and said "Get out, imperialist swine."

The $250 000 satellite system was set up at an angle of exactly 47° to the satellite and Alan called home to test it. He got...an answering machine. ⋀

The team at Basecamp. Everest looms in the background. Back row, from left to right: Lhakpa, Mike Sullivan, Ang Nema, Ang Temba, Alan Norquay, Myk Kurth, Jamie Clarke, James Nelson, Ross Cloutier, Mario Bilodeau, Bill Noble, Hilda Reimer, Timo Saukko, Denis Brown and Pat Morrow. Front row, left to right: Alan Hobson, Ang Tsering, Tim Rippel, Peter Austen, Jim Everard, John McIssac and Dawa.

CHAPTER 9

Basecamp Luxuries

I was attending an educational staff meeting somewhere in Canada. My eyes were gently closing. Everyone appeared to be a huge cardboard cut out. They were all talking at once in mega-jargon about some educational topic. "Integrated incremental parameters are being systematically implemented." Images of Nazi rally movies and the cut outs saying "Ve haf vays of making you tok" wove in and out of my mind. The vivid blue and white colours of the tent hit me right in the eye. The snow was piled up and a small disembodied hand reached into the tent. There was a tin cup on the end of it and a pale liquid steamed into the tent.

I was dreaming. But which was the dream? I spilled Sherpa tea and knew I was on Everest. We were to have a high altitude disease and drug briefing session in fifteen minutes. While we all had a pretty good knowledge of this topic, Denis, in his chirpy style, brought everyone up to date: "Morphine can not be used for head injuries or when a patient is unconscious."

"So you can't ever use it, eh, Denis?"

Tim volunteered his wife Becky to go into the Gamov bag which Mike, our high altitude specialist, demonstrated. Mike looks like a medical Groucho Marx, and there was always a touch of humour in his explanations: "If your wife is not cooperating at 24 000 feet, put her in the Gamov bag. Pumping up the bag by foot pump if you are at, say, 24 000 feet will reduce the effective altitude pressure to 15 000 feet, and she will then do anything you ask."

The meeting continued with rescue techniques and a master

plan for logistics on the mountain. We decided that the team needed thirty-two oxygen bottles out of forty-eight to get eight climbers to Camp Six at 27 000 feet. We would have to establish five intermediate camps over six weeks' time to reach Camp Six. At approximately 25 000 feet, even the best of climbers need to use oxygen. The air is just too oxygen-poor for human functioning. We would use the remaining sixteen bottles to get four climbers to the top. Denis and I rigged up the metal detector which we had borrowed from Tom Holzel in Massachusetts. We would use this device to try to locate Mallory's camera. If we could find Mallory's camera, we hoped, it would have summit shots in it. The film, experts agreed, would be preserved, albeit in delicate condition. We wanted to develop the film on the mountain to prove that Mallory had been the first on top. Combing the campsite produced buried vintage tin cans and metal bars, but no 1924 cameras.

When Mallory was on Everest in 1924, he was thirty-eight years old. It was his third expedition there. Away from Everest, he was a schoolmaster who did not like his job. While he liked the students, he had difficulty understanding why he could not be human and treat them as equals without their taking advantage and walking all over him. His energies went into Everest instead. I knew how he felt.

His climbing reputation allowed him to be picked for the first-ever Everest attempt in 1921. After this trip he was so politically involved and personally driven that he found himself on Everest again and again.

Mallory had a reputation for being somewhat haphazard and making quick decisions. On his last attempt his team included Odell and Irvine. Odell, a much more experienced climber than Irvine, was very well acclimatised. Irvine was only twenty-one and a very fit rower who had proven himself on expeditions to places like Spitzbergen where he had made the first crossing. Mallory took Irvine with him on their last, fateful attempt on Everest in early June 1924. If Mallory had chosen Odell, the outcome may have been very different.

Previously, I had discussed Mallory's effort with Tom Holzel, who has amassed much information on the mystery, and made his own expedition to Everest in 1986. Because the weather was awful, his team reached only 25 000 feet. They did uncover some new evidence.

Holzel told me that the Chinese had climbed Everest in 1960 by the Mallory route, but, because of their conflicting reports, no one in the West believed them. Holzel took their photographs and by computer analysis proved that these pictures could only have been taken near and on the summit. Because of this, the CMA let Holzel, on his last day in China, talk to the tent mate of a Chinese porter named Wang who had discovered a body at 27 000 feet. This porter was subsequently killed in an avalanche. The tent mate told Holzel that Wang had found an "English" close to his tent. This body was found 1 000 feet below the point where an ice axe had been found in 1938. In fact Holzel had predicted that a body would be found in the same area. Wang touched the clothes of the body and the preserved, but somewhat decayed threads of tweed blew away in the wind.

Holzel was convinced that this was Irvine who had been instructed to return to the North Col while Mallory took the remainder of the oxygen and went for the summit. Irvine, a novice, probably slipped, leaving his ice axe behind and falling to his death a thousand feet below. Likely this is what happened since when beginners fall, they are so surprised that they forget to use the axe as a tool to break the fall.

Mallory continued toward the summit. For him, it was "death or glory." He couldn't return to England without achieving Everest's ascent. England needed heroes, alive or dead. Mallory, in my opinion, carried on the English tradition/mania for death-defying heroes from Captain Scott, who didn't return from the South Pole because of poor planning and bad luck. England's fascination with "death or glory" adventures knew no limits. For example, Amundsen, a Norwegian who beat Scott, a Britsh subject, to the North Pole in 1912, addressed the Royal Geographical Society after his success. The chairman, by derisive implication, called Amundsen's attempt "unsporting" because he used dogs while Scott had pulled his sledges by "man-hauling." Mallory was part of this national masochism.

Once reaching the summit of Everest, he tried to make it down in deteriorating weather, took refuge on a ledge and died of hypothermia. I think he is still there. No one of the thirty-five or so people using his route and suffering from "summit fever"—the desire to reach the top at all costs—has had time to look for him. Sir Edmund

Hillary reached the top in 1953 and told me he saw no sign of Mallory's passing. However, the 100-mile-per-hour winds could easily have obliterated all signs. However, being optimists, our team was all set to have a look for Mallory and find the camera.

I went for an acclimatisation walk up the Rongbuk Glacier one afternoon. When I returned to camp, knowing that Mallory was notorious for misplacing things, I casually said, "I found this old box thing under a boulder. Does anyone know what this old box with a tiny hole in the side and the initials G.L.M. [George Leigh Mallory] could be?" There was a lull of wonder and revelation until the rest of the crew realised I was pulling their leg. If Mallory's camera were to ever be found, it would clear up the longest and most enduring mystery in the mountaineering world.

It would almost be equivalent to finding the *Titanic* if it could be proven that Mallory was the first to reach the top of Everest. In his 1922 attempt Mallory and others reached the North Col. On one trip up they had set out too early after a snowstorm. Avalanches occur most frequently immediately after a storm as the snow has not had a chance to consolidate, a process which takes several days. Mallory

The ice pinnacles of Rongbuk Glacier.

and his Sherpas were avalanched and he watched, horrified, as seven of them were overwhelmed and killed. This put an end to the Everest attempt that year. In 1924, a memorial cairn of three thin slabs was built to commemorate these Sherpas and others who had perished on the mountain.

I had formed an idea where this cairn was situated from pictures in old climbing books, but the six-foot-high cairn had been knocked down and disappeared before 1938. The expedition in that year found no trace of it. I searched the area for a whole day as part of my acclimatisation schedule, turning over old slate rocks, brushing off the lichen and dirt. Towards the end of the day, I found one and only vertical piece, leaning against a rock. On the back of the piece of slate, perfectly preserved, was the name PEMA. Excitedly I rushed to get the book with the best picture of the old cairn and there, right in the middle of the page, was the name PEMA. I had a piece of mountaineering history in my hand; it had lain there for sixty-seven years.

That morning was set for our first personal calls on the satellite system. My wife Kay phoned on August 8. She could tell from the call just how much trouble I was having breathing. She told me I sounded like Darth Vader with laryngitis. My fertile brain conjured up some images from the movie. The "dark side" was the rarefied atmosphere and the awful nagging headaches. The "force" was the willpower needed to remain up there and not to head back for lower, more pleasant altitudes.

John and Denis took off up the mountain with the Easter Island statue to see how high they could get. They rolled into camp eight hours later, after having reached 21 000 feet as well as being drenched crossing the Rongbuk River which was in semi-flood. Himalayan rivers are very treacherous. The year before, the leader of a Japanese expedition had been swept away and drowned.

Several of us braved the three river crossings where the river split into swollen streams, treacherous with afternoon snow melt. Here we found the memorials to the many climbers lost on Everest. And there were many. Boardman and Joe Tasker were two of Britain's boldest mountaineers who in 1982 had tried the "last great problem" on Everest, that of the pinnacles. These are the great rock outcrops on the lower part of the north ridge. They were last seen at 27 000 feet.

Joe Tasker's movie camera was later found below the pinnacles, but unfortunately there was no film in it to show what may have happened.

Other notable disasters have occurred. Marty Hoey was a strong climber who slipped out of her climbing harness while on the North Face of Everest and fell 5 000 feet. In 1988, a person I had climbed with, Roger Marshall, fell down the Japanese Couloir to his death on the North Face of Everest, during a solo attempt. Rudiger Lang had been forced to retreat from K2, the second highest mountain in the world during a horrific storm in 1989. In the spring of 1991, he was trapped by the wind high up on Everest. Two of the Sherpas who accompanied us had watched as he sat immobilised at 26 000 feet while the unrelenting Everest wind drained his life away.

Why do people do this crazy activity? Do we all suffer from a sort of collective, divine madness that makes us go to the ends of the earth and put our lives in jeopardy? The answer lies in the beauty of the heights and in soaring above the mundane. Nothing beats standing on the summit of a lofty peak after incredible, but in hindsight, satisfying effort. Drinking in sights that so few are privileged to see seems to compensate for the danger of losing one's life.

I find, however, that as I get older there are many lower mountains in much warmer climates as well as many other areas of endeavour to be savoured. This really does temper my ambition to climb the highest peaks in the world. I think of what I would be missing if I were dead. And I will be a long time dead!

Thoughts like this made me careful and humble on the highest mountain in the world. Many climbers want only to reach the summit at all costs, being driven or, in modern parlance, totally goal-oriented. They lose sight of the joys of the journey, but I was determined to enjoy these.

On August 9, we awoke to nine inches of fresh snow. This was the day when the monks from the Rongbuk Monastery formally blessed our expedition. The monk who had ridden up with us made some strange looking sculptures out of dough. Together with these, he placed the food that we had given him. The Sherpas strung up prayer flags which fluttered over the camp. They lit a juniper fire. Such a blessing is important as the Sherpas would be hesitant to continue without it. Their sense of spirituality affected the team who stood around sombrely for the first hour while the monk did his incantations. We all secretly wondered if we would actually be returning to Canada or be leaving our bones behind on the mountain.

Chanting, the monk threw first rice, then flour in the air. Some accidentally hit Myk Kurth. The monk smiled so Myk impishly threw some back. With the usual Tibetan humour, the monk started laughing. Soon we were all involved in a low-key food fight which relieved the spiritual tension. Who says religion can't be fun? No one in the East seems frightened of Buddha. They seem merely respectful and appreciative of his humble presence. No one in the West ever thinks of the Christian god as having fun. It's all too serious stuff, this preparing for the afterlife. Myk said to me afterwards, "People are so friendly here because they have so little and nothing to protect materially. Death is so close for them all that they have much compassion towards all mankind." I tended to agree.

For the next while we continued to acclimatise and have small seminars while Hilda cooked for us. It was a low-key, relaxed time when having fun dominated. For example, someone mentioned how

The blessing.

muscle mass rapidly depleted at altitude. Mike punned that "muscle mass" must be weight lifters going to church in Italy or Ireland. For the serious business of extremely high altitude climbing, we had a constant-flow oxygen system as well as an on-demand one. No one could agree which was the better system, so to be safe, we brought both. Timo had designed a system whereby the cylinders could be zipped into a rucksack.

We spent another whole afternoon doing promotional shots for our sponsors. Getting good photographs of 20 people in a group is tricky. Coordinating clothing and getting everyone to smile at the same time is not an easy task. It either requires a public relations genius or a second Hitler. Because Al has a German background and was team manager, we delegated him to organise it. The machine gun he had installed on the hill above turned out not to be necessary. The most memorable shot is one in which all of us have popped our heads down inside our expedition parkas. The effect is that of 20 outdoorsy Anne Boleyns.

The Chinese jeep had taken some of our "trekkers" back to Zhangmu, but, three days later still had not returned. We were

Anne Boleyns for a day. Goof-off at Basecamp.

relieved to see it come round the bend into camp to take out our remaining friends and relations. It was a tearful farewell for all of us. How many would return? No one really knew.

I had been very leery of allowing non-climbers come to this height with us as many hikers have died in the high mountains from altitude-related problems. These deaths could have been prevented if a rapid descent to low elevations were possible. Unfortunately, it is not possible from Basecamp. We had been lucky no one had been seriously ill, so we heaved a relieved, but sad, sigh when the last trekkers climbed into the jeep for the trip out. To ease our strange feelings of loss and excitement over the coming challenge, we spent the next day doing "real" work: packing 100-pound loads for the yaks to carry.

Up above Basecamp were some rocks that looked as though they would offer some good climbing practice. Climbing difficult, technical rock is strenuous at 18 000 feet, but the sunny day and views of the North Face of Everest made up for it. The climb was good acclimatisation practice for us.

One of the other teams at Basecamp, an Indian expedition, had just had a radio message from their Advance Base Camp (ABC) saying that all their fixed ropes had been avalanched—over 2 000 feet of a complicated rope network. Members of this team had already been at ABC three weeks. Some of their climbers had been even higher. They had reached 24 000 feet on the avalanche-prone North Face where the average angle was about 40 degrees. As avalanches are most common between 25 degrees and 55 degrees, the climbers had been very lucky.

While the Indians were climbing on one side of the great gully, an avalanche had hit the other side. So a few days later when they climbed back up, they used the old avalanche track because it would likely be safer. Their leader was Pranesh Chacraborti and he had a restrained but warm old world charm. He referred to his team as "our boys and girls." Whenever I meandered over to his tent to check on his team's progress, his sister, also a very good climber, would act as a gracious host. She would give me peanuts and incredibly strong coffee which made my eyes feel like they were ready to leap out of my head at the ends of little springs like in the cartoons. Caffeine and altitude combine for strange effects. While Al would usually pound me at chess, I had the edge on Pranesh. He would lose graciously with a big smile and a "well, them's the breaks" look.

By this time just about everyone was settling in to Basecamp while trying to get higher. I walked up the Rongbuk Moraine, the stony outflow of the glacier where we had super views of Pumori, Lingtren and Nuptse, the sites of previous epics and tragedies. We tried to reach the Lho La, the Col between the Khumbu Icefall and the Rongbuk Valley, but the river coming from the East Rongbuk was too high. The only access was via a long detour round a precarious ice cave which had giant icicles crashing down at regular intervals. We decided to leave that climb for later and opted for Xarlungnama, a peak which guarded the approach to the East Rongbuk. Alone I reached 20 000 feet and felt fairly light-headed.

On the way down I noticed a strange, heavy apparatus made of iron and wood. It was a tripod of a very old design and in a strategic position looking up into the East Rongbuk Valley. It may have been an old tripod of Captain Noel, the official photographer and cameraman of the 1924 expedition. I was reminded of Noel's part in the tragedy. At the end of the 1924 expedition, when Mallory and Irvine disappeared, Noel told of how he went into the Rongbuk Monastery where the senior Lama used his fabled brain power to project a blurred image on the wall. What he projected was Mallory and Irvine descending from the top. They were just below the summit when Irvine fell in a hole. Mallory then fell in. Noel kept this story to himself for many years as he thought no one would believe him. Finally he told it to Brian Blessed, an English actor who attempted Everest many years later. In 1991, the tripod was too heavy for me to move and, as far as I know, it is still there if anyone cares to look for it.

On August 25, I rose at the crack of noon at Basecamp and feasted on the strange breakfast of three eggs and kippers. I have found, at high altitude, the foods I like have to be salty, savoury or natural, like eggs, fruit, or potatoes—of which we could never get enough. My appetite was so depressed that the idea of a particular food really had to appeal to me before I would eat it. Even chocolate, for which I normally have a manic craving, couldn't arouse my interest.

Prowling around the camp there were ravens, pigeons, hares, and choughs in the stream area. It felt like a national park in Canada. Watching the pigeons' antics, I thought to myself that they must get spinal problems from their constant jerking to and fro. A few yaks had wandered on to the hillsides across the river and there was a small dog with them. It walked exactly like the yaks, head down near the ground and placing each foot very carefully.

"Probably having an identity crisis," I thought.

Al asked the Sherpas if we could get some "yak milk." When they stopped laughing their big toothy laughs, a very puzzled Al asked what the joke was. It turned out that only the female *naks* give milk.

Yaks are neat animals. They are a relative of the North American bison. They cannot exist at altitudes much lower than 12 000 feet. Your average, western cow has a mixture of curiosity and timidity but timidity takes precedence. Yaks have this attitude too, but they are quite indifferent to people. They will only respond to their own driver who motivates them with a strange mixture of grunts and whoops.

But yaks can be fierce if threatened. Moving extremely fast, they can demolish a tent with their horns in five seconds. We learned to keep out of 'hornshot' at all costs or risk getting skewered, as happened to one innocent tent. The Tibetans use the soft yak hair for cloth and the coarser outer hair for mats and tent coverings. They

Our Chinese guide Mr. Li (left) and our interpreter Louis at Basecamp.

make saddles, whips and boots from the hides. They use the bushy tail as a fly chaser on the warmer days.

Going uphill or downhill, yaks maintain a steady pace of just over two miles an hour. We had to be very fit in order to keep up with them on a steep uphill section. For their bulk, they are uncanny in their ability to walk on ice, boulders or knife-edged terrain. I never saw one slip.

We had established Advanced Basecamp, and we watched as the thirty yaks leisurely rolled into Basecamp to be loaded. I asked Lhakpa how long it would take to reach ABC. He startled me by singing, "ABCD, EFG, HIJK, LMNOP." He must have learned this from a previous expedition. He then told me with a straight face that the yaks have headaches above 21 500 feet and that's why they cannot go any higher than this. It was an interesting point, but it didn't answer my question. Λ

CHAPTER 10

The Fight for the North Col

The evening phone call from the advance team came in loud and clear. Denis and John had already established camp at 21 000 feet. They were preparing the glacier with fixed ropes over the crevasses. We wondered how their food supplies were holding out, as they had been up there for several days. Their situation brought to mind more off-the-wall humour.

This time it is a Monty Python sketch in which there are several sailors marooned at sea and they are starving. The captain says, "You'd better eat me because I have a bad leg and I'm going fast."

Another sailor says "I'd rather eat Johnson, Sir." So they all decide to eat different bits of each other. We wondered which bits of our lead climbers we would lose before the yaks got the food up there in the next three days.

The yak drivers left about 1:00 p.m., after waking up at noon and rearranging our carefully-done-up loads in a style that would better suit the yaks. Several of us accompanied them. We walked for two hours and then camped one hour further up the East Rongbuk in a wonderful situation. The hiking to this point would have made the trip worthwhile even without the allure of reaching the top of Everest.

The Tibetans pitched their black soot-encrusted tent, and soon yak-dung smoke poured from the hole in the top. The herders were well organised. This was a local industry controlled by the head men in villages which were about fifty miles away. Unfortunately of the exorbitant fees the CMA charged, the yak herders got only about one tenth of one percent of the $8 000-per-guide fees that we paid.

We pitched the tents quickly, as the usual afternoon storm was upon us. The mornings would usually be cloudy; then the sun would come out and melt the previous night's snow. Towards 4:00 p.m. a huge black wall of weather would appear in the distance and no matter where we were, we would head for shelter. It would then rain and blow and finally snow. This was the typical pattern at the tail end of the monsoon.

We picked our way through the Rongbuk Moraine through dips, rises, pools of ice water and boulders. As we looked back the yaks would appear and disappear constantly in the varied terrain. Lumps of ice and boulders would drop from above as the hot sun warmed the mountain up. High peaks shimmered all around. The mountains were so high it was hard to estimate true scale. We reached 20 000 feet. As Mike, Bill, and I felt sluggish we decided to stay put for another day to recuperate. Bill, our second cameraman, was ecstatic about the photographic and filming opportunities. The ice towers all about us had fantastic shapes and were up to fifty feet high.

I went looking for Maurice Wilson who was a crazy, obsessed Englishman who had this idea of making his first ascent of Everest in

The yak herders greet us.

the 1930s. As he could not get permission to go to Everest, he taught himself to fly. He refitted an old Tiger Moth biplane, took a few climbing lessons and flew to India, an amazing feat in itself. He disguised himself as a monk and somehow wangled his way into Tibet. He had this weird idea that if he fasted, he would gain the spiritual means and physical ability to climb the mountain. He had no idea of the horrendous conditions on the mountain, nor did he have any climbing ability.

In spite of these drawbacks, he still reached the amazing height of 23 000 feet, living on next to nothing. Worn down by the unrelenting conditions, he died in his tent. Some years later the famed British explorer Eric Shipton found Wilson in his tent and pushed his remains into a crevasse. In 1960 the Chinese found him for a second time at the lower altitude, and buried him. Some people have speculated that this body may have been Mallory but the clothes were too modern. Also Mallory vanished at 28 000 feet, much higher than the glaciers' end at 23 500 feet where Wilson was found. It is doubtful that any fall could have caused Mallory to be found as low as this.

Some people may find my interest in the past adventures and tragedies morbid, but I don't. Looking for artifacts of past adventures is like examining the middens of North America.

I challenged the yak drivers to a stone throwing game to see who could demolish the tops of the nearby ice towers. They were fearfully accurate at twenty-five yards and rightfully proud of their prowess. To show how we admired them, we gave them lots of our food like soups and biscuits, both of which they really liked.

While acclimatising at 20 000 feet we received a radio call establishing that the advance team was well on the way to the historic North Col. Here I also discovered exciting skills, previously unknown. My mechanical aptitudes were so developed that I managed to fix the yak driver's flashlight with a wad of paper and a jammed-in screw.

It was very hard to sleep that night because of a continuing suffocating feeling caused by the high altitude. But the day at 20 000 feet helped us, and the following day we took off for Advanced Base, reaching it in a growing storm with the temperature at -10°C. The yak drivers had carried seventy-five pounds and still kept up with the rest of us who were carrying only twenty-five pounds.

The next day was hot and sultry, amazing for 20 500 feet, and the six inches of new snow was gone in two hours. Avalanche conditions high up were very bad and no one had dared set out that day. I read *Fear and Loathing in Las Vegas* from my stock of books. That crazy lifestyle and those frenetic cities seemed a long way away from Everest. That night it snowed again and thundered. It was hard to distinguish the snow slides from the thunder and occasionally I would lie there in a panic wondering if that last boom was now heading across the valley for me. A huge roar right behind my tent made the tent rock and I waited for the impact. Nothing happened. Then the sleeping pill hit and I woke up next morning, looked out and saw the remains of a slide a yard thick and zero yards away. It had come off Changste, the north peak of Everest. The whole team was now at Advanced Base on the 5th of September at close to 21 500 feet. Everyone was fit and no major health problems were evident.

After a major snowstorm we had to wait two days for the snow to consolidate and as snowstorms often happened, progress was awfully slow. The advance team of Denis, John, Mario, Tim, Mike and the Sherpas had fixed ropes up to half way to the North Col. In the main tent that morning, Mario related how he thought the last night's slide had caught him but then he realised it was a mouse running over him. The mice were constant night companions but all they did was chew toilet paper. Two ravens showed up. We suspected these to be the ghosts of Mallory and Irvine. Their calls were so deep they sounded like jazz xylophones or water in distant pipes.

Even at this height, the garbage from past expeditions was truly staggering. It was most apparent at ABC with oxygen cylinders, tins, propane tanks, and miscellaneous junk scattered about. Many countries were to blame. It is the same all over the Himalayas now. At Nanga Parbat Basecamp 200 blood sample test tubes were left by a German expedition. Very few people seem to care. There have been clean up enterprises but the problem is worsening, although Basecamp is better now.

I wrote in my diary that night "snowing like crazy again. The mountains here have a mind of their own. I woke up and heard Mike Sullivan's cough in the tent next door." We all had our own tents at Advanced Base as we needed the private space. Poor Mike had been trying to reach the North Col for several days, but every time he set off at 5:00 a.m., his bronchitis would get the better of him and make him vomit. His frustration level was evident.

Most of us had some minor ailments ranging from sinusitis, colds and coughs, to bronchitis to diarrhoea. I remember waking up once with my bowels being very insistent that I get up immediately and run to the latrine trench. On this occasion I didn't make it, and I sat down on the moraine to cry before doing an emergency wash.

I got my usual sinusitis when the cold air damaged the lining of my nose. The infection worked its way into my sinuses and my nose would not stop running. The Sherpas called me Peter "Nasperay" or Peter, "the Dripper."

Advanced Basecamp
at 21 000 feet.

The problem at altitude is to prevent ailments from getting worse. The eagerness to go higher conflicts with the need to look after yourself, so you do not become really sick. It is a tough mental battle. With an all-male team, stoicism can be a problem. I saw one of the team throw up on the way up to the North Col. He did not say anything and pretended it hadn't happened. Even if a person is sick, he does not want to appear as if he is not pulling his weight. Therefore, he tends to hide any illness unless it is really bad. Thus he gets sicker.

I think western competitiveness is to blame for this. My attitude was simply that if a person did not want to set out that day, the rest should trust his judgment. He should feel no compulsion to go. He shouldn't need to justify his actions all the time. Even with this approach, people pushed themselves too hard. For example, when James came up to Advanced Base, his retinas started haemorrhaging. He still suffers some loss of vision as a result.

John, Denis, Jim, Tim, and Mike, who were feeling pretty healthy, went up back to the front line, fixed some rope over a very steep section, and retreated to camp. However, the line proved to be too dangerous; they all went up the next day, removed the ropes, and fixed them further left. The fixed ropes allow climbers to move themselves and their gear by using clamps, called jumars, on the rope.

It snowed and howled that night. We waited two days before the main team went up again only to find our fixed ropes buried under two feet of cement-like snow. It took a strenuous day to extricate them.

The following day dawned clear and cold. We watched from the camp as the team, with Dawa Noodle in the lead, plowed a large furrow up through the new snow, on a sometimes up to 60-degree slope. Six hours after setting out, the lead pair of Lhakpa and Dawa pushed laboriously on to a hundred feet below the North Col. Denis, Tim, Myk, and John followed them.

The Sherpas are fine and powerful climbers in their own right, although they do it for a job. How much joy they derive from it is open to question. I think they believe westerners are nuts to come all this way and pay mega-dollars just to flog themselves to death carrying loads up a mountain.

Four of us watched breathlessly as the team moved incredibly slowly in the dangerous, avalanche-prone cement-like snow up the almost vertical section to the North Col. They were there—without mishap! Another huge step forward had been completed. We hugged each other as if we were soccer stars. How would we fare on the next, just as serious, step?

The next day I skied over to the Raphu La for a look at the East Face of Everest, the Kangshung Face. It was horrific. The Americans had fixed ropes up the first 2 000 feet of overhanging and extremely difficult rock on their first attempt some years ago. They then came back two years later to carry on. They reached the summit after six weeks of effort. One climber wore only his underwear on the top, it was so warm. He reported it was still enough to light a candle on the

*The infamous
North Col.*

summit. In contrast, when I saw The East Face, it looked like the jaws of hell. This was the face for which I had received permission in 1986 but refused. I'm glad I did. I remembered that Boardman and Tasker were lying up there somewhere after falling from the pinnacles on the North Ridge.

While I was again wondering why I do this stuff, one of the Sherpas, the one we nicknamed "Answering Service," brought me back to reality. "Peter Nasperay, let's go back. Weather getting bad." Indeed it was. We rushed back to the comfort of our big Habitat tent, and some French fries— an uncalled-for luxury up here.

So far, we had some gear on the Col, and it included food and tents. It was obviously going to be a fight with the weather all the

Practicing above ABC,
over 21 000 feet.

way. We were also being lulled into a false sense of security because when a climber makes it up difficult terrain safely once and even twice, the really intense fear wears off to merely heavy uneasiness. In fact, we could be wiped out at any time to which the sixty or so unwilling ghostly guests on Everest would attest if they could.

Mike and I discovered some great rock climbing above the camp. It was all good acclimatisation. I was excited as I figured I was well enough acclimatised to attempt reaching the North Col. The pattern was for climbing parties to alternate day by day, depending on who was fit. My brain was staying cleverer than Mike's as I was ahead in chess games, whereas we had been level a week ago; so I thought I should have a try. My nose was running and my chest was hurting, but I figured now was the time.

Ravens are lucky for the Sherpas; and our mascots, Mallory and Irvine, constantly swooped over and into the camp, often dive-bombing the tents, looking for food. They would perch on a rock with heads cocked on one side and appeared to be sitting down. They seemed to say, "okay, guys, we're ready to order. I'll have the tuna melt and my buddy here, the omelette. Thanks, no hurry. We have all the time in the world." No one dreamed of hurting them, and if we had the Sherpas, I'm sure, would have gone home.

I popped half a halcyon, the sleeping pill. I know they are bad for the system, but without them there was little sleep. At 5:00 a.m., I woke up to the hiss of snow on the tent. My hopes rose. If it snowed more than four inches at night, giving the threat of avalanches, we could doze on. I stuck my finger in the white cover outside. "Blast, only two inches." I wanted to go, but it was agony to leave the warmth of a beautiful warm down bag to venture into the cold of an Everest night despite the seductive lure of the world's highest summit.

It was so awful to leave the gorgeous sleeping bag that we took leaks into bottles we took with us to bed. The penalty for missing was dire, however; one felt like a ten-year-old who had just wet his bed. Letting the other matter drop, though, was a different proposition altogether. We did all we could to minimise exposure of the tender parts. If we were in for a prolonged stay at the latrine, there was a definite risk of frostbite when the wind raged and the temperature was low. Unfortunately, the cold and discomfort tended to delay the whole process. Often the body cowardly refuses to deal with the elements and demands a more user-friendly environment. I actually suffered slight frost nip to my butt, although I did not become aware of it for a while.

Ablutions accomplished, I dragged my unwilling body towards the Col. The headlight on my helmet flashed off the new snow crystals, making them look like a million glow worms. My 50-pound pack felt like a 200-pound boulder. I stumbled along. It took five breaths for each step on the 50-degree slopes. The problem of cold feet arose when we had to stop to catch our breath. My feet froze solid three times, and I had to swing each foot 100 times to rewarm it each time. Not enough oxygen was entering my circulation system to reach my extremities. I heaved a sigh of relief when the violet hues of the sun crept over the horizon and lit up the slopes. I took my socks off; my feet basked in the sun's radiation. The toes said "thank you" in unison, and I knew they meant it. Now we had to peel off three layers of clothing to fight to stay cool as the temperature went from -20°C to 20°C.

Mario, Mike, and John were going fine, but were puffing like steam engines. We weaved in and out of huge icicle-encrusted crevass-

The North Face dares us.

es, and peered into bottomless black pits. Ice towers menaced us from above. It was like *Jack and the Beanstalk,* when Jack first ventures into the giant's castle after his climb up the beanstalk. Like him, I was spellbound but full of healthy fear. Sweating and panting, I reached Dawa's Chimney just after Mario. I jumared up the rope, and plopped on to the Col like a fat, landed fish. The North Wall of Everest hit me in the face. It seemed so close, but might as well have been a universe away even at this altitude of 23 500 feet.

We could clearly see from the North Col the First and Second Steps and even the rock band where Irvine had supposedly been found. They were all tantalisingly close and beckoning, like the famous Lorelei Rock in the Rhine River, where a maiden reputedly lured sailors to their deaths in the Middle Ages.

My radio burped and Alan Hobson came on. "Pete, What is it like to have reached the North Col after all these years of hassle and preparation?" I was close to tears from having got this far and being so close to my goal. I mumbled something about the amazing other-worldly experience I was undergoing.

Then Alan said, "Here's your wife, Kay." It was wild. I had just plonked myself on the North Col and, telepathically, my wife knew. This was the highest and first Canadian telephone call—ever—from Everest, and I was part of it.

Kay said, "We're all missing you terribly, and the media have been calling me for news of your progress at all hours, and I can't get any work done."

I wheezed some reply about having them phone us direct and how was Gorbachev doing in exile? and was my son Glen behaving? and I'll bet the weather here is worse than in northern British Columbia and then the line went dead. The signal had travelled 72 000 miles and almost three times round the world.

It was a pretty historic moment for me. I was standing on one of the main focal points of Everest climbers. To think that Shipton, Bonington, Messner, Smythe, Mallory, Irvine, and dozens of others had all stood here within a seven-foot radius of where I was presently standing. I hugged Mario. He was pretty pleased too; his big grin just shone out like a beacon. Jim Everard, already on the North Col, was also grinning from ear to ear. "Amazing place, eh, Pete?"

It was hard to speak. Everyone wanted just to soak up the ambiance of being there. Now seventy percent of the team had made it to the North Col. I buried my load of food in the snow. A big mistake. I should have put it in a tent but, was too happy to think. The ravens got it. We strongly suspected that it was Mallory and Irvine, our friendly neighbourhood reincarnations, which had devoured the lot.

On the way up, I had noticed something underneath a cornice, or overhanging piece of snow. Now I could see it was a tent, upside down. The wind had caused the snow to roll over the years, and this tent on the North Col had been thrown where it still hung years later like an old wasp's nest. It was inaccessible, so there could be no adventure to determine its history.

Tim had been on Mt. McKinley in Alaska, earlier in 1991 to prepare for Everest. While pitching camp on a ledge, he had found some clothing sticking out of the snow. Digging down he unearthed a macabre scene. Three Korean bodies, missing since 1965, came to light. Mountains do sometimes give up their secrets.

Looking over to the great couloir, or gully, on the North Face, I could see the Indian team at its high point which was about a thousand feet below us. They were perched on a tiny ledge. Their camp looked highly precarious, just to the side of a huge avalanche path. Their route had been first climbed by Everest's first Australian expedition a few years before. That team had made the ascent without artificial oxygen but some team members were badly frostbitten. It was a tour de force, as they climbed a totally new route. Unlike the conditions for the Australians, the Indians had permission only for the monsoon period of July and August. In attempting the climb in these conditions, they were exposing themselves to high risk.

The route up the North Peak of Everest, Changste, looked relatively easy and short. However, distances up this high are deceptive, as they are foreshortened. This route had in fact been done by an Argentinean climber on his own a few years ago. His was a highly dangerous undertaking because if he fell off the ridge there would be nothing to stop a 3 000-foot free fall into Nepal.

In fact, something like this happened on a Belgian expedition in the 80s, a climber on the south side of Everest in Nepal vanished near the summit. His partner returned alone. Everyone had given the one who had fallen up for dead; but a week later he turned up back in Nepal, at basecamp, having somehow worked his way round the Lhakpa La, a high pass overlooking the Khumbu side of the mountain. He informed the amazed onlookers that he had fallen, in a storm, all the way down, but he couldn't remember where. Miraculously he found himself unhurt!

I guess it can happen. A friend of mine once free-fell two hundred feet to land on a pile of rocks. He broke both legs, arms, and pelvis, but still crawled to the highway in four hours before he passed out. There have been some unbelievable falls in mountaineering. A German team fell all the way down the Triolet north face in the French Alps. One climber was killed, but the others escaped the 2 500-foot fall with bruises.

At the beginning of my climbing career, I was climbing in the French Alps with an Austrian, Karl, an extremely tough and grizzled old climber. We were descending in a storm. Karl was using the rope to rope down or rappel, but it was attached to an ice pin of dubious worth. The pin pulled out and he free-fell for eighty feet, bounced on the glacier, and disappeared, accelerating into the fog for at least three hundred feet. I was terrified and ran down after him, thinking no one could survive a fall like that. I found him in a heap, and motionless. He moved and shook himself. No injuries! It was nothing short of miraculous.

Another friend of mine, climbing in Yosemite in California, fell ten feet, hit his head, and died. If a day has your number on it, I guess that's it. I still think you can lessen the risk by prudent planning, though.

The five of us headed down from the North Col. We had lost track of the time, being so spellbound with the place. It was already noon, really too late to descend with any peace of mind. We went anyway, cutting it rather fine while keeping an eye on the ever-melting seracs and the softening snow. A serac is an ice tower which can range between ten and five hundred feet in height. It is in constant movement on a glacier and can drop on you at any time. Myk Kurth skied the slope, falling only once in the process. As the slope is at an average angle of 45°, this was quite a feat. We made it back to camp without mishap, but sunburned and exhausted from all the exertion at this ridiculous altitude. One member had preceded us and went back on his own, against my instructions. I had wanted us to stay together in case of accident. People were, as I knew would happen, bending under the strain and behaving unpredictably. This was all right to a point, if no one else was affected. ⋀

CHAPTER 11

Disaster Averted

That night, to celebrate, we feasted on rich banana cream pie and crepes-improvised-suzettes. The Sherpas had us share their "tongba," a fermented devil's brew into which everyone stuck a bamboo straw and sucked hard, while one of the Sherpas stirred the gunge on the surface. Despite the description, sucking up tongba is a very soothing process which creeps up on you, belts you on the head, and transports you benignly to the land of nod. The Sherpas did this every night that they could, getting "raucous" by their quiet Sherpa standards. They would play counting card games with the climbers. Their favourite climbers were Tim and John, who got more tongba this way and hence grew more philosophical. It also made them forget the dangers of the day and allowed them to look forward to tomorrow.

The expedition was beginning to feel like a way of life. I felt I had always been here, striving for this elusive goal. The days were coalescing into one enormous ethereal experience. You can become accustomed to anything. How do prisoners feel in jail for years? Time telescopes and becomes meaningless. You can only relate to it through memories of what you know.

Homesickness comes to the fore no matter how seasoned a traveller you may be. You long for not just familiar but for intimate faces. What was Kay doing now? I knew our relationship would be even better when I got home. "Absence makes the heart grow fonder" outweighs "out of sight, out of mind" by far in my experience.

Would we make it? No one knew. The mountains are harsh and

fickle mistresses, especially this one—Chomolungma, the Goddess Mother of the World.

The next day I woke up to snow blowing in every direction. Visibility was reduced to zilch. I started to formulate this theory that the more snow there was, the less oxygen was available, because the snow absorbed it to stay fluffy and snowy. It just felt like that. When it snowed, I found that breathing was harder. Psychological? Claustrophobic? Who knows? All I knew was wheeze, wheeze, lie down, and breathe deeply before panic set in.

Boom!

"Al, was that an avalanche?"

"No. It was a raven dynamiting the food cache on the North Col."

"So that's how they do it."

We were pinned down. No one could venture out in the driving blizzards. Everyone was quiet and contemplative. The Sherpas, very observant, watched us closely to see how we would tolerate the close confinement. Occasionally someone would get tired of the claustrophobic conditions of the main tent and retire to his private tent to read or sleep. We had a game of film title charades. Try doing *Attack of the Killer Tomatoes*. It requires almost as much acting ability as a Neil Simon play.

The camera team interviewed everyone for their thoughts so far, plans after Everest, weather, food, diseases, hopes, chances, homesickness, chances of success, discovery of Mallory, lapses into schizophrenia, and related brain damage. The time of waiting lacked the relaxed fun of acclimatising at Basecamp. After all, we were pinned down in a blizzard 21 500 feet up. Our world was a series of tents, one large communal one, and smaller, private ones for each of us.

Sounds of life were the taps of chessmen, the whoosh of snow, as well as the blips and burps of too much prepackaged food as it moved through our bodies. These sounds were played to the accompaniment of the sniffles, the coughs, the crazy Sherpa songs—a mixture of East and West—and the inexorable wind.

To leave the tent we had to put on more clothes. If we weren't moving to create heat we tended to look like the Michelin man. If one of us went outside, stumbled and fell over, he resembled nothing so much as a turtle. He would roll on his back, arms waving as he tried to extricate himself from the deep snow while fighting for breath, thus mouthing like a leatherback turtle.

The avalanches cracked, whooshed, and crashed at regular intervals. I went into hibernation and finished *The Master of Ballantrae* by Robert Louis Stevenson. There is a part in this book where the Master has been killed and buried in the wilderness for weeks. However, when his servant finds him, he is amazingly still alive, having learned about suspended animation in his travels in the East. The avalanches falling all around made me wonder what white burial would be like. I hadn't been in the East long enough to learn the art of suspended animation. I gloomily remembered that when the head is fully buried up to the mouth, a person only has two to five minutes to live. People who have survived burial in avalanches say it is terrifying; others have had near-death experiences and felt liberated. I didn't want to find out.

Reading the *Tibetan Book of the Dead* was scary on Everest. I can recommend it only to someone really into horror and fantasy. The book does gives some insights into reality, though. A departed soul is described in this book as rushing into any state of being—a reborn human being, a beast, an unhappy ghost, a denizen of hell—anything rather than the "burning brightness of unmitigated reality." My reality here was totally unreal. I continued to escape reality into classic literature. A mouse, nibbling toilet paper, brought me back to semi-reality.

To break the monotony, we tried to make James feel better about the retinal haemorrhages in his eyes. So we goofed off, crazily play-acted. The scene was reminiscent of an old *M.A.S.H.* episode with Hawkeye and B.J. crazily and inventively on a roll. We had a major goal, as did the doctors and the soldiers in *M.A.S.H.* Our ailments were not as serious, although some writers have compared climbing on Everest to being in a war zone without a rifle.

Basecamp called us twice a day at set intervals. They relayed the calls from home, really helping our morale. Ashley Ford called us from *The Province.* "Did you foil the emerald smugglers yet?" We looked back on our relatively civilised time in Kathmandhu and laughed. The media had become interested in our progress, but until something sensational happened, I knew from previous experience, the interest would only be minimal.

Mike Sullivan had given up; his bronchitis was bad and getting worse. Before he returned to Basecamp, he made us all a surprise: rum and eggnog. Beeootiful!

Finally, days later, the weather was better. I trained my binoculars on the North Ridge of Everest, above the North Col, as six of our team including four Sherpas struggled to 24 200 feet, as measured by their Swiss-made altimeters. They returned to the Col to stay the night and acclimatise at a higher elevation than ABC. The dilemma was this: we had to acclimatise by sleeping higher but this made us deteriorate faster. We had to balance these two factors, as well as the weather against the risk of becoming too exhausted to perform.

We called North Col from ABC. John said Denis was suffering from food poisoning, probably caused by a prepacked meal with a crack in its wrapper. We were amazed that botulism could survive so high. Eating and drinking were definitely problems. We were supposed to drink at least four litres of liquid a day, but we had to force ourselves to do it. Denis was immobile and had been throwing up for hours. He thought he was on the verge of kidney collapse and he should know, being the doctor. The rest of the team forced him to eat and drink liquids, and in two days he recovered enough to return to ABC.

When the climbers returned, we discussed the possibilities of trying the Ershler Variant which crosses the North Face close to the Mallory route and takes a later, but direct line, to the summit. This variant is named after Phil Ershler, a climbing guide in the States, who reached the summit on his own a few years back by this route. His climb is another great example of courage and single-mindedness. But after our discussion, we decided to stay on the Mallory route. Better the devil we knew than the devil we didn't.

Next morning saw Alan Hobson and me drinking sweet Sherpa tea and eating porridge in the cold gloom of the cook tent. We set off at 5:00 a.m., on September 15, planning to spend the next two nights on the North Col. There were still six team members on the Col, doing their level best to stay warm and keep their spirits up in their snowy eyrie. As we left, it was bitterly cold, about -15°C, and almost moonless. Clear skies have a greater cooling effect up there than at lower altitudes. The snow crunched gently as we lumbered up the moraine, each alone with his own thoughts which were the usual fare: "Why am I carrying this monstrous lump on my back? Why am I doing this? What am I doing here? Why can't I breathe?"

I felt like Captain Kirk from Star Trek, who, whenever he got stuck on another planet with aliens always came up with the same daft questions: "Who are you? What do you want with us? Why can't we go home?" It was as if he expected everyone in the universe to have the same friendly, reasonable "earthling" outlook as he had. His questions would never really be answered. My questions were similarly absurd. The next day there we'd be toiling up the moraine with the same questions roiling around inside our head.

I had come to know and respect Alan even more over the weeks. His professional broadcaster manner had put some of us off at first. Behind it all, he was a very unassuming, and caring person. He was usually the first to enquire how someone was feeling, and everyone appreciated his genuine concern. As a writer, he could define and pinpoint people's characters pretty quickly. This ability of his helped me understand the team's changing behaviour patterns and interactions.

For example, some climbers became more intense as our dilemma grew while others got crazier with *M.A.S.H.*-like humour. When sense of humour is lacking, things, in my experience, get way too serious, and you stop enjoying yourself. You can enjoy yourself in spite of the horrendous effort of carrying heavy loads at 24 000 feet. I tried to convey that spirit to the others.

As we trudged onward to the North Col, the dawn came up and with it came every imaginable violet tint. We stopped to take pictures at the high cache at the foot of the North Col. Captivated by the scene, we failed to notice the wind rising to a low whistle. I put on my overboots and crampons, but by the time I had this done, my fingers and feet felt frozen. If I ignored them, frostbite would set in. Time for 100 tiring swings of each foot. Sensation in the feet returned, but so did the wind which had crept up to 20 miles per hour.

We stomped around trying to decide what to do while the wind rose to about 50 miles per hour. The temperature was now the equivalent of -70°C. Windchill lowers only the feel and effect of the outside temperature; it actually stays the same. However, when you look at the thermometer, you would swear that it should dramatically plunge down to -70°C. The wind was howling and knocking us over. I said to Alan, "It must be horrendous on the Col. If we carry on up the ropes, we'll be fully exposed to the wind." Because my feet had already been frozen, it would be even worse for me this time.

Alan agreed. "I'm disappointed, of course, that I can't sleep on the Col but as I have been there four days ago, it's not so bad. Live and fight another day." *Carpe diem.*

The feathers of cloud in the wind 4 000 feet higher up on Changste were fantailing out for hundreds of meters. It looked hellish. There was no movement on the Col. The guys were wisely not stirring from their bags.

There was nothing to be done in this wind. The winds blowing off Everest and down the Rongbuk Glacier are legendary, but this wind was too consistent; it was like the force in a wind tunnel. It was ominous. I wondered if the upper atmosphere jet stream winds which regularly whip the mountain in winter were dropping down early. The height of these winds was right; the main bulk of the wind was blowing at 26 000 feet and above. These winds, too, have an Everest tragedy. The Japanese climber Kato climbed Everest solo in winter, but on his return the jet stream wind blew him into oblivion. Neither he nor his camp on the upper slopes at 27 500 feet were ever seen again.

We turned and headed down to the relative paradise of ABC. About half way down, I looked over to the rock wall of Changste. There, fallen over and leaning against the wall was a white cross. As usual, my ferreting and archaeological instincts kicked in. It turned out to have an interesting history.

I went over, taking care to watch out for stones falling from the towering rock bastions above. I cleaned up the wood of the cross. The wood turned out to be from Brummie Stokes' expedition of several years ago. He and Bronco Lane of the very tough Special Air Services Division (SAS) of the British Army, unsuccessfully tried the difficult Northeast Ridge. Later, a Chilean expedition found a packing case with British Army marking, a piece of the earlier British team's garbage, and used it to make a memorial for a fallen climber.

The body underneath the carefully rounded grave turned out to be Victor Hugo Trujillo who had died on August 16, 1986. The Brazilian team which was on the Everest mountain at the same time as we were told me that Victor had been wiped out in an avalanche half way up the North Col. His team had brought him down this far to be laid to rest. He was twenty-two years old. Sixty people had shuffled off this mortal coil en route to the North Col. Sobering thoughts.

We had been lucky so far; seventy loads on the Col indicating seventy individual trips. Think of the potential for accident! Even one death profoundly affects the morale of everyone on the mountain. I cleaned up the grave and tried not to weigh our chances. Despite my attempts, I reached ABC with my mind firmly ensconced in thoughts of our mortality. Our presence on the mountain was definitely speeding up the possibility of an expedition to the otherworld. More fatalistic climbers have often said to me, "Well, you've gotta go sometime."

My reply is "Right, but why speed it up?"

In a long push two days later to Camp Five, some of the team placed a tent and some equipment at 26 000 feet. They took care to put the food inside the tent. Did ravens get this far? The winds had

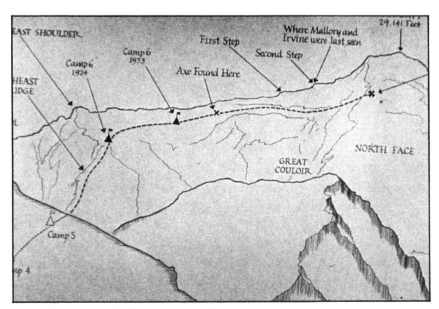

Map showing the Mallory route on Everest.

moderated enough to allow a concerted, but exhausting effort to struggle to Camp Five. Then suddenly it happened. We had the media's full attention.

Tim was happily moving ahead at 25 500 feet a couple days later, going up to our high camp. He was feeling great. I was happy because I had always thought he had the drive and ability to grab the summit. He was now spearheading the attack along with Denis, Mario, and John. On the return trip, he broke through a patch of hard crust into soft snow. This pitched him forward and twisted his knee. He was in great pain and limped his way down, with lots of help, to the Col. As he knew he was probably finished with the climb, his injuries must have seemed that much worse.

As he was not able to get off the Col himself, we started a major rescue. Luckily, the weather was fine and there was little wind. We have long pondered the results of this accident. On one hand, if this accident had not happened, the day could have been used very profitably to get us higher. On the other, getting higher could have been dangerous because climbers would have been pinned down at a high altitude with no way of moving up or down in the wind. Maybe this event was providential in that it spared us from further mishap.

John, Mario, and Myk rigged up a system to lower Tim who was in a morphine-induced dreamland. Roped and bundled into an "Everest improvised" stretcher, Tim skittered down an icefall. It was straight down a vertical section of the North Col where, in all probability, no one had ever been before. Ross, Denis, Pat, and the Sherpas went in from below to catch him. Our only control over the rescue were the ropes attached to his stretcher/sled. All these manoeuvres took a lot of time; the day wore on, getting warmer all the time. Thus, the snow was increasingly unstable. They lowered him the first 150 feet on ropes which had been attached to ice axes hammered into the snow. They then had to attach two more ropes. It was a complicated procedure that climbers practice regularly as there is a lot that can go wrong. Tim was to be lowered close to 1 200 feet to safety.

While these new ropes were being attached, one of the jumar clamps and connected slings did not catch. A jumar, when moved up a rope and weighted, will jam on the rope. A sling is connected to it. Tim's ropes were lowered though a system of clamps. Mario had to hold a rope with his bare hands. Despite his painful yet determined grip, the rope slowly slipped through his fingers— almost to the end. Luckily he was strong enough to manage to hold it until John got the new rope attached. Tim was contentedly oblivious to the fact that his life was literally hanging on a thread. I was with Bill, the cameraman, watching and filming from a distance. Innocent of the danger that had occurred, we happily took advantage of the "photo opportunity."

The rescue scenes on the video are gripping as Tim bounces his way down the most dangerous part of the North Col. Pat and Denis are seen moving across to grab Tim as he appears again lower down. Caught up in the drama of the rescue, they did not think to rope up, forgetting there were crevasses in the snow. Their mistake.

Pat fell seventy feet into a sloping hole and Denis fell in afterwards. Luckily they escaped with no injuries, since crevasses kill many unsuspecting people and climbers round the world every year. They are one of the leading causes of mountain accidents. The fact they were not injured allowed for a little joking around later and it reminded me of Bowman's classic spoof on Himalayan climbing in *The Ascent of Rum Doodle* in which a climber falls in a crevasse. Everyone is anxious; when they establish communication with him, he says he is fine, and to "send down champagne." A rescuer goes in after him and another message comes back up to "send down more champagne." The next message is to "send down a song book."

Being deep in a crevasse, especially unintentionally, is an incredible experience. Green and blue or multicoloured and latticed ice shimmers eerily all around. You feel you have died and either gone to heaven or to another planet. The feeling of unreality can be terrifying. I once fell fifty feet in a crevasse in the Columbia Icefields in the Canadian Rockies when a partner inadvertently crept up to where I was on the edge of a crevasse. He had forgotten that the rope must be tight to stop his partner going in if and when a snowbridge collapsed. I remember feeling, "This is it. It has been a good life, but this is how I am gonna go." Just as the rope went tight, I jammed in the constriction, as crevasses are hour-glass shaped. I managed to climb out.

Emerging back into the bright sunlight and 25°C after the icy gloom below and -20°C was like coming back to life. I do not want to be morbid and I'm not preoccupied with death or anything, but by a strange twist of fate my mother passed away that same day. I think she somehow protected me. Weird, eh?

On another occasion, an acquaintance of mine wasn't so lucky. He was on skis, not roped, fell a hundred feet, and died of exposure before his partner could rescue him.

Back on Everest, the time was 2:30 p.m. and it was now obvious the rescue had been started too late for comfort. Whoosh! A medium-sized avalanche came down 20 feet to the left of the proceedings, fortunately missing everyone. It was not that large, but all death needs is a thin covering of snow and ice. I was reminded of the famed alpinist, Dougal Haston, who made the first ascent of Everest's Southwest Face. He was killed in a tiny avalanche which hit him while he was out for a solo ski on a spring afternoon in Switzerland. He was barely covered but still could not extricate himself in time to avoid suffocating.

Tim finally reached the bottom, with the the help of the Sherpas who took over from Pat and Denis. Everyone rushed up to see how he was. He was cold and dazed. We sedated him again with Bailey's Irish morphine, a little-known narcotic. We improvised a ski sled and Tim

Tim at ABC after his rescue. More pain killer seems to be counter indicated.

was whisked off to ABC to sleep off his ordeal. He was diagnosed as having torn the cruciate ligaments in his knee, very painful but the diagnosis was he would recover in a couple of months.

The next day was "Climb for the World Day," an event originally organised in England, but now celebrated worldwide to draw attention to the deteriorating environment of the planet. People were climbing in every country to raise awareness. On this particular day, we were proud to be on the highest, most desirable climbing goal on the planet.

Poor Tim, nicknamed Timberline, was still in great pain and couldn't move around much. Alan and I took Tim's ski poles and improvised crutches, using great technological expertise, moving from one engineering discovery to the next until we had a working model. Tim tried our much-heralded units and they collapsed on the first hop. Some modifications were speedily made, however, and he could scoot around somewhat. To "speed" his psychological recovery, we spent fifteen minutes doing Long John Silver—the one-legged villain of the movie Treasure Island —impersonations, but going "ARRR OOO ARRR !" gave us sore throats pretty fast.

We had put out a message about the rescue to the media in Canada and were then bombarded with calls from newspapers and TV stations all over the world. They did get Tim's initial statement right, "I don't know where the pain is—in my heart because I have to turn around and go back—or in my knees." However, some of the headlines were emotionally overdone and distorted. The media seem to need this type of material to maintain their sales. For example, one headline read, "Family Wants Hurt Father off Everest." Another article had half the rescue team being avalanched and then falling into a crevasse!

Well, there was no harm done and the rescue more than anything else raised Canadian awareness of the expedition and, by association, Rett Syndrome. Becky, Tim's wife, talked to him and Cathay Pacific Airways kindly offered to fly her out to Kathmandhu to meet him. Our problem was to get Tim to Kathmandhu. The first stage was to get Tim to Basecamp. While most yaks will not allow people to mount them, we had asked the yak herders to find one that wasn't user-surly. They kindly brought one up who did indeed seem to be a benign animal. He stood there, quietly waiting.

Tim's leg was immobilised and he was strapped in the wooden saddle for the long, painful ten-hour ride down. Mike Sullivan and I also decided to go down; Mike because his bronchitis was worsening, and I because I couldn't stop my nose from dripping all over the landscape. We were turning into hypochondriacs. I also had oesophagitis, an inflammation of the gullet which makes it hard to eat or swallow. Even without this new affliction, I was finding it hard to eat.

Mike and I re-evaluated our strategy. We decided the best strategy to get up Everest is to spend a week at ABC, go higher, but then drop down to Basecamp. Once we felt better at Basecamp, we could then shoot for the top in one long push, if the weather permitted. On our way down, a backward glance revealed ominous long streamers of cloud blasting across the upper part of the North Face, although elsewhere the sky was mostly free of cloud.

Tim rode in drugged amazement as the yak "tip-hoofed" gently over knife-edged icy ridges. Going down a steep slope Tim would lean back, with his head touching the yak's hindquarters. Tim did a super job of keeping his spirits up although he was in great pain and must have been very disappointed. I'm sure Tim will return to Everest just as soon as he gets another chance.

It was great to return to Basecamp for a well-earned rest. It was September 23, the 69th anniversary of the first ascent of the North Col in 1922. Had that first group's conditions been harsher than ours, I wondered?

We caught up on happenings among those who had remained at Basecamp. James was in good spirits, but he still had some vision loss. The central macula was damaged and the medical opinion is he will probably always have some sight loss. The 4 000-foot altitude loss meant we could breathe again, much easier, but any recovery was probably illusory. We were still higher than the highest settlement in the world which is at 17 000 feet, but the psychological value of being "down" at Basecamp was very "high," though.

The first Brazilian team to attempt Everest had just moved in to camp. Each time I walked past their camp, I eyed a big tub of potatoes which called out, siren-like, "Eat me." Some tea-drinking and friendship-making secured us enough for four loads of fries. We luxuriated by the stream, all afternoon, stupidly fat, full and semi bovine, or yakine, to stay geographical. This was a real change from the isolation of ABC.

We negotiated with the Chinese to get Mike and Tim out to Lhasa. The jeep ride was going to cost $500 US each. Then there would be further untold sums for the flight to Kathmandhu. The Chinese agreed to take the men out along the route by which we arrived. With luck, there would be no more landslides. Canada called that night at the prearranged time to say that Becky would be in Kathmandhu to meet Tim when he arrived. Ⱥ

Another view of the forbidding North Col.

CHAPTER 12

Waiting it Out

enis came down for a rest to recover from his food poisoning but no one else came down. The others remained at ABC to catch a break in the wind if one came. The plumes over the summit were miles long. The wind was increasing to hurricane force. There was no movement on the mountain.

While we luxuriated amongst the pleasures of Basecamp, some fascinating people came through. One or two came on a privileged trekking tour; others had smuggled themselves into Tibet. Most notable of the latter, "Barry the Guru" or "Tex" was a strange apparition, about six feet tall, with pebble-like glasses. He wore a bizarre hand-knitted Tibetan toque which he never took off. He insisted on cleaning up Basecamp and singing with James, Jamie, Denis, Alan and me. For this, and because he pretended we could sing, we gave him food and some clothes.

He was in rags. His footwear consisted of black pump material held together by holes of different sizes. His sleeping bag was useless; a gunny sack dating, I am sure, from the Spanish-American War. He had been in Tibet for three months hitchhiking around on army trucks. Because he would not allow photographs of himself, an apocryphal story arose that he was a Texas chain saw massacre perpetrator on the run from a maximum security jail in Texas.

He had wangled his way to Lhasa. All westerners are supposed to be on officially accompanied trips once inside Tibet. However, if by some inexplicable means, a person can make it to Lhasa, he can obtain a Tibetan visa with relative ease. Such are the ways of the highly-evolved Chinese bureaucracy.

When arriving at a customs checkpoint, "Tex" would show the guards pictures of semi-clad ladies. These were very hard to obtain in prudish China. His actions worked as a natural passport. But if he had had completely nude pictures, he may have been slapped against the wall and shot. On the other hand, he may have been made a sergeant. I wouldn't want to take the chance. While "Tex" was not a climber and was very ill-equipped, he obviously had a great sense of adventure. I would meet him again on my second return to Basecamp from Advanced. I saw him at about 20 000 feet, when he was toiling up toward ABC, against everyone's advice. A bad storm would have killed him but he made it, returning a few days later to Basecamp with blisters and sunburn, in a state of complete exhaustion. Fascinated by the Mallory story, he wanted to see the scene of events that happened so many years ago. I'll bet he's still in Tibet.

Another group passing through Basecamp was a French trekking group who needed Denis' services. Their leader had phlebitis of the leg, a condition which has to be treated immediately or would lead to dangerous blood clots. One of their party had ventured on to the lower slopes of the North Col and found an ancient Russian ice piton, similar to the ones we had seen on our earlier expedition to Russia.

The climber's find made us aware of yet one more bit of Everest history. Rumour had it that a team of thirty or so Russians had vanished on these slopes in the 1950s, but the Russian and Chinese governments never confirmed or denied the story. Communists do not fail; therefore the attempt never happened.

Other interesting visitors to Basecamp included Ken and Emily Ransford from Denver, who had been in the East for six months. So far, their main adventure had been a long, arduous raft trip along some unnamed and isolated river in Indonesia. They described the feeling of putting the raft in the river, taking off in the current to who-knows-where yet being aware at the same time there was no going back. Their trip sounded like something out of a Joseph Conrad novel.

The next group to tramp through involved one of those travel coincidences for me. They were British. One of them was Ted, aged 69, from Yorkshire, in England, with an accent like that of the farmers immortalised in James Herriot's *All Creatures Great and Small*. For some reason, he had no trouble with the altitude. I entertained him with war songs. "Ee, by gum, a 'aven't 'ad so much fun since Secind World War. Wunderful, it is." The others, I guess, you would call the "landed gentry." Their accents were Oxford English, straight from the drawing rooms of genteel Mayfair, a very rich and famous area of London where most of them, in fact, lived. They had one or two titles: "Sir," "The Right Honourable." One of them, Michael, a lawyer, was heir to Lord Aberconway's Welsh estate, Bodnant Gardens, which resembles Butchart Gardens in Victoria.

Now, it just so happened that in my student days in the 60s, I was standing with my wife Kay in the driving rain, in the middle of nowhere, hitchhiking to Wales. Suddenly this Jaguar Mark 10 screeched to a halt, the door flew open, and a languid voice said, "Hop in." We dived into leather-lined opulence, the like of which I had never seen before. We discussed Italian art all the way to Wales. At the time I had my doubts about the privileged classes in Britain. However, Lord Aberconway turned out to be a very gracious, warm-hearted person. Meeting his heir on Everest somehow seemed appropriate.

Until this point, we had not realised James could cook so well. He made everyone deep-fried shrimp for dinner. We had a wonderful time. I suggested he go as a cook on his next expedition. It was great to be away from the tension of the trips up to the North Col. Three days later, Mr. Li returned from escorting Tim and Mike out. He brought vegetables and, glory of all glories, beer. He informed us that Tim and Mike had been dropped at the border. As far as he knew, the road had been re-established through the landslides. Tim and Mike should have made it back without any problems.

We learned later that Tim arrived back in Canada to a hero's welcome, receiving more press coverage than anything about the expedition so far. Human suffering in danger-laden circumstances draws the press like nothing else. I have often thought of starting a "Good News" newspaper, since I am thoroughly sick of all the doom and gloom reported in the press.

While recovering at Basecamp, I went exploring the old Rongbuk Monastery site as well as the hills and caves behind it. A gaping hole would invite me into it and the possibility of discovering old Tibetan artifacts excited me each time I went into a new cave. I found many altars and clay tablets from centuries ago. The tablets fascinated me most of all. The monks dug out clay, made tiny clay tablets using casting designs and left them deep in the caves. The tablets gradually decomposed into dust. Today, monks continue this process to signify the eternal presence of the gods.

On our last night at Basecamp, I dreamed of a furry something on my forehead. I woke up and on my forehead was a mouse, probably asleep, using me as an electric blanket. The next day, Alan and I took off back to ABC, feeling well refreshed.

When we arrived, we learned that Camp Five was in at just over 26 000 feet. Eleven climbers were sitting tight, in a howling gale, on the North Col: Denis, Mario, Myk, John, Timo, Jim, Ross, as well as the indomitable Sherpas. Jamie had gone up two days beforehand, taking advantage of a lull in the wind, and fulfilled his dream of reaching the Col. Alan Norquay had a problem with his foot; he couldn't bend it upwards and had been told to stay at ABC until his foot was better.

Alan Hobson and I walked up to Camp Five, feeling fairly strong

Jet stream wind whips climber on Everest.

and with high hopes because the wind was blowing only in strong gusts. Approaching our intermediate camp at 20 000 feet, we could see the streamers crazily blowing off the summit. Other than the streamers, the sky was crystal-clear. All the monsoon snow was gone from the faint trail leading up through the moraines.

We piled into the little emergency tent in the camp and found a tin of crab left for us by the Canadian team who were on Changste, the North Peak of Everest. While people might have expected rivalry between two groups vying for their country's attention, there was none. We got along fabulously.

They had worn themselves out carrying heavy loads to the base-point on Changste. They had not negotiated beforehand with the Chinese for yaks to move their gear. Once they arrived in Tibet, their liaison officer was totally inflexible, refusing to give them any yaks at all. They attempted to deal with the yak herders privately and obtained a few, but when their liaison officer found out he cancelled the arrangement. In contrast, our liaison officer Mr. Li had been very accommodating.

Two hours from ABC, we met Jamie who was returning for good to Basecamp. As both our communications experts, Jamie and Alan were not in camp, James was handling the two daily calls to our camp on the North Col.

Large chunks of ice fell from the slopes of Changste and startled us into watchfulness. We had been dream-walking our way up. One hour from ABC, the clouds thickened and snow flurries started up. Rounding the last bend before the last steep section to ABC, I saw the downward tracks of the Changste team rapidly filling in with snow. They had made a wise decision in quitting the mountain.

As night fell, I reached the big tent. Alan followed me in half an hour later. The big hugs from the Sherpas made us feel that we had established a happy family over the relatively short time we had been together. Hot food and warm smiles made for a snug oasis in the storm. The wind buffeted the tent sides and threatened to rip our fragile home off the mountain. I increased the number of stones on my tent guy ropes and read some Sherlock Holmes. The raging wind outside was blowing over a landscape a mere 20 000 higher but even more desolate than the barren moor where the evil eyes of the *Hound of the Baskervilles* gleamed. That scratching sound coming over the moraine? Was it the Hound? No, it was another mouse.

The radio call that night from the camp on the North Col established that most of the team had had enough, after braving the winds on the Col for days. All but Denis, John, Mario, and Myk had come down. Myk had a quasi-Buddhist premonition of danger and had strange feelings that he shouldn't be there. He descended. Because Myk had a reputation for going on at all costs until conditions made it impossible, this was unusual. Altitude has peculiar effects on people. I thought Myk would be our "secret weapon" to reach the top but it was not to be. The wise Sherpas felt there was little chance left to reach the peak, but we climb mountains for adventure, right?

As long as there is a slight glimmer of hope and a risk that can be calculated, even minimally, climbers will go for it. Mallory went for it on his third try but pushed too far. I had to give up on my dream of finding traces of him high up I had found traces of his expedition, but it was obvious that a really concerted effort to find him would have to be made by an expedition solely dedicated to that task. It takes a superhuman effort to attempt Everest. We discovered we simply did not have the time or the resources to look for Mallory as well as try for the summit. In the end, all our efforts were geared to simple survival. In the mountains, the discoveries are by happenstance.

Given the conditions, hindsight suggests it would have been a good plan to have established a camp at the 25 000-foot level on good ledges instead of going from 23 500 to 26 000 feet in one step. As it turned out, this 2 500-foot distance was too far and too exhausting in the snow conditions. As well, we were carrying 60-pound loads. With a camp at 25 000 feet, climbers could have rested at this intermediate camp and gone on or turned back without feeling each attempt was their "last chance".

Imagine the feelings of our run-down climbers as they, bone-weary, looked out of their tents. The next camp was over a mile away, 3 000 feet higher, on a slope that averaged 40 degrees upward. Imagine, too, the effort that would take in atmosphere that had 60 percent less oxygen than sea level.

Mallory was certainly on Denis' mind when he looked out on the wind-swept slopes of the North Ridge on the morning of October 1.

The ledge where Irvine was presumed to rest lay 4 000 feet above and was plastered with snow, probably hard-packed. If we got that high, the chances of finding him would be very slight; besides, we had laid that quest aside.

Ross had discussed the climb with John, indicating that he had given up the climb and wanted the rest too, out of safety considerations. Our intention, he said, always had been to avoid leaving bodies on the mountain. His responsibility to ensure we all remained alive and reasonably healthy outweighed his motivation to have the team continue. He thought because the wind was not subsiding, any further movement was inadvisable.

Others of the team had decided against going higher for various reasons. I had bleeding sinusitis, and blood circulation problems which caused my feet to continually freeze; Al still had his feet problems; James had his eye problems; Alan had altitude problems; Myk had motivational problems. Tim and Mike had gone home; Jim and Timo thought it was too risky with the weather, as did the Sherpas. I could have ordered them to continue, but I felt everyone should be able to choose for himself.

Time was running out. We only had a week or so left before the yaks would return to ABC as had been agreed, and we had learned the lesson of keeping CMA-sanctioned teams waiting. Unlike the rest of us, John, Denis, and Mario were still fit and motivated, felt that time was running out, and wanted to go higher, even at great risk to themselves. The conflict I had wished to avoid was here. Some wanted me to cancel all further movement. Others said, basically, "Go for glory. We'll never be back." As overall leader, I had the veto and I was in favor of adventure. I left it up to the climbers to carry on if they chose to. I knew that they were capable of reading the conditions. If they were unfavourable, I knew that John, Denis, and Mario would have the sense to turn back.

As most climbers scorn the status quo, given a chance to go for the summit of Everest,they would go for it, regardless. To deny these three their chance seemed cruel to me. Despite our carefully worded contract which said the team members would abide by my decisions, I realized that when the summit beckons, many events can happen. I thought of Herman Buhl.

He was another of my boyhood heroes. Indeed, I had lived in Austria for five years following in his footsteps. In the early 50s, he made the amazing first ascent of the 26 000-foot Nanga Parbat in Pakistan in an incredible solo effort lasting 42 long hours. This was one of the most unbelievable mountaineering ascents of all time, up to then. It was against the wishes of the expedition leader who deliberately snubbed Buhl when he returned. The legal implications were complex, but they pale before Buhl's legendary fame among climbers. I decided to allow the "Buhls" on my team to have their chance. Λ

Looking down on Pumori in Nepal.

CHAPTER 13

Risking It All

The wind had died down and I suspected I had the same feelings that Noel Odell had had when he looked up and saw Mallory and Irvine on the upper ridge, disappearing into the void. The three of them—John, Mario, and Denis—were moving ever so slowly, about fifty feet apart, each seemingly lost in his own thoughts. They had had a council of war the night before and weighed up the chances. They were on their own, but pulled each other along with their mutual enthusiasm. They could take only two cylinders of oxygen per person. This, together with the food and personal gear, was cripplingly heavy but unavoidable. I watched their snail's progress until they vanished on the other side of the ridge. As they disappeared, I wondered if I should call them back on the radio. As expedition leader, I was responsible for sending them to what might be certain death. I couldn't stop them. If I were fit enough, I would have been up there, too.

Re-creating their experience from later conversations, I imagine it was something like this:

Conversation takes a lot of effort and none of them had the energy to spare. Only the odd rope command interspersed with heavy panting broke the silence. John was light-headed. Mario mentioned his feeling of a strange mixture of trepidation and exhilaration. Denis believed they had a chance, but felt tentative about an attempt because the wind could return at any moment and trap them high up. In 100-miles-per-hour conditions, a climber cannot move. He can, in fact, be lifted bodily and deposited wherever the wind may take him.

They plodded upwards for hours, pausing to start an oxygen flow at a low rate. If they were economical with the oxygen, it might just get them high enough to go for the top. They didn't worry about the descent because if a climber makes a high summit like this, he usually does not need oxygen on the way down.

Placing one foot in front of the other was all they could do. Denis wondered if he would ever return from this no man's land of ice and snow. As they mounted into the region called "The Death Zone," above 25 000 feet, they had to ignore their fear of the unknown and concentrate on merely putting one foot after another. After three hours, they felt as though they had made no progress on this great, white whaleback. In the rarefied atmosphere, unreal conditions, and attendant

The push for 26 000 feet.

hallucinations, their one touch-point was their personal commitment to each other. The rope cemented their camaraderie. They were the spearhead of our attempt on Everest; the culmination of years of effort.

The black and curvy crevasses at the foot of the North Face, looking like shark's gills, grinned mockingly some 3 000 feet below to the right. The wind rose, threatening to pitch them over into the 4 000-foot abyss on the left. The wind did lift Mario off his feet. It, capriciously, as if it had a mind of its own, ripped off John's sleeping bag, which had been attached to his rucksack, like a piece of paper. He watched, horrified, as the bag arched at high speed into the void, a disappearing red speck. He knew that to avoid frostbite he could not sleep at that height. To go to sleep this high without a sleeping bag meant he would not awake. Even having the will to keep warm is a major problem. Climbers have to constantly admonish themselves to remain awake and alert when they feel themselves sliding into apathy or high altitude lethargy. There has been only one exception. Doug Scott and Dougal Haston made the highest ever bivouac with no sleeping bags at 28 700 feet on Everest in 1975. They rubbed each other's feet all night and sustained no frostbite. They had to have been physiologically exceptional; for the rest of us, such an adventure would mean certain death.

The Indians' camp of one small tent, at 24 500 feet on the North Face, was now far below. It occurred to Denis just how puny and insignificant it appeared on this huge vertical surface. The camp would be wiped from the wall in a second if the Goddess so much as sneezed. Denis and his fellow climbers kept on, fired by the thought that, if the wind stopped they could get higher, to the camp, dig in, reach the ridge next day, and possibly—just possibly—go for the top the day after. It was a long shot but they had the willpower to carry on. They need up to five breaths for every step. They had to pause every ten seconds or so. A slip would mean death. Just the thought of a slowly accelerating slide to the edge of the ridge and then a free-fall to those crevasses made a sixth sense for survival kick in.

They reached the vicinity of Camp Five, semi-exhausted. There were clear skies and a raging wind. Where was the tent? It was late and dark. The snow was too hard and too shallow to dig a snow cave in order to hide from this relentless wind. They searched the whole area, becoming desperate yet managing to avoid life-threatening feelings of panic. John could feel the cold creeping insidiously into his body as it sapped his control of his limbs and sapped his willpower. The steady-flow oxygen helped.

I knew exactly what he meant when he told me later of his feeling that he could not prevent the cold, caused by the wind, from seeping into his body. Finally, the three of them had to conclude that all had been blown away: tents, oxygen bottles, extra sleeping bags, food, even the Prince George flag for the summit! In short, everything was gone.

As they looked at each other, their faces mirrored their fears that they would not make it back alive. White patches indicating the beginning of frostbite began to show on their cheeks. Their only option was down as fast as possible. There was no discussion. Team telepathy made them unanimous. It was almost dark, and the wind was more than a full gale; it was a horrible shrieking, living force, trying to tear them from the mountain. They had to ram in their ice axes and hang on, waiting for a slight lessening in the wind to allow them to stand up and try a few steps. They couldn't talk because they had to save strength and because the wind was too loud. Each of them knew the trip down, not the trip up, was to be the terrible fight for survival. They were operating in an equivalent temperature of -80°C. John told me of the indescribable weariness which came over him, but he managed to keep going as he knew that to stay that high in that wind would have meant certain death. Mario knew he had to keep going or face dying, but still felt his feet slowly but surely lose their feeling. He knew he would sustain some frostbite but did not have the energy to take any measures that could prevent it.

Giving up on Everest must have been a difficult decision indeed. John made himself think of his family. Thinking of his individual family members, he would do two steps for each them for hours to keep from giving in and sinking into the storm. Denis, by his own admittance, was terrified, and concentrated on his crampon spikes. Catching a crampon in one's clothing can pitch one forward and have dire consequences as many an unsuspecting climber has found out. Experienced climbers as they were, this was still the most harrowing night any of them had ever spent. Five hours later, around 3:00 a.m., they collapsed, totally spent, into one of the few remaining tents on the North Col. The powerful winds had ripped the rest off the mountainside.

We received no radio call from them that fateful night; I feared the worst. They had simply not thought about phoning, being so preoccupied with surviving. They slept the sleep of exhaustion. When Denis woke up, he couldn't believe he had survived the night. We continued to work at the radio. "Come in Denis. Come in." There was no answer for hours, but finally a feeble, cracked voice mumbled: "We're safe. Send up eggs Benedict and coffee." They were okay! We danced, whooped, and hugged each other in relief. The cloud of doom lifted. We knew all chance for the top had gone, but somehow no one cared. We were a big expedition on the highest mountain in the world. We had no serious injuries. I think I heaved the biggest sigh. ⋀

The Lhakpa La where Mallory first saw the North Face of Everest.

Epilogue

he three summiteers rested on the Col for a day and rolled into camp, looking like emaciated Egyptian mummies. There was a difference, though: these men were alive. It was October 6, my birthday. Hilda baked a cake to celebrate my birthday and our incredible adventure. We had all been close to the gates of eternity, some closer than others, but all had lived.

Many people are obsessed with climbing a particular mountain. They speak only of the hardship. They forget to appreciate the splendour and experiences of the journey. It was not so on our trip. It had been a kaleidoscope of unreal experiences, fantastic people in many countries and astonishing, visual delights. The hardships were nothing compared to these wonders. There was disappointment, certainly. Not reaching the summit, as Denis said, was merely a symbol for the continuing struggle to find a cure for the Rett Syndrome. Finally the media had become interested in the life-and-death struggles of Denis, Mario, and John, our final pared-down team, and this, combined with Tim's rescue, raised awareness about Rett Syndrome in Canada and worldwide It continues. As you and others buy this book, another dollar pours into research into the Rett Syndrome.

We cleared the Col of our gear over the next two days. It was an awful job for the Sherpas and for those few climbers still fit enough to go back up. All knew there were to be no more attempts. The yaks came and everyone looked forward to the pleasures of Basecamp, but the Goddess didn't give up. The winds still raged high up and buffeted us all the way back to Basecamp. We tried to console ourselves thinking that at least fate and the mountain did not laugh at us by stopping the winds once we had abandoned our attempt.

There was a party that first night at Basecamp. There were many grades of refreshment from Chivas Regal, ten, to Chinese brandy, one. Everyone pulled out their hoards of liquor, chocolate, and comfort foods. Tension we had felt for months, even years, lifted.

Mario mentioned that in Quebec "We ski in Chicoutimi." Myk thought he said "Whiskey in jacuzzi, me?" Several people noticed that hair grew less at high altitudes. We teased that Jim didn't have a problem, since he was pretty thin on top anyway. We even had a food fight lasting about ten seconds. Mario got covered with chili sauce, I got plastered with lasagna, and the interior of the tent looked as if it had been decorated with raspberry ripple ice cream. As the fight started, ten people scrambled together for the eighteen-inch-wide door. The yak herders stared in amazement, as we all piled out of the tent, like a Monty Python rendition of parachutists on a mission behind enemy lines.

That night, James, Jamie and I spent a happy hour with Cassin, the lead yak herder with whom I had struck up a friendship, and several of the other herders. They tried to sing our songs, a word or two at a time: "Swing low, (sweeing law!), sweet chariot, (sweeet cheriod!)." We stretched our mouths round their high pitched, haunting melodies. The asphyxiating yak-dung smoke filtered the stars shining through their tent-top opening as we split our sides laughing at their verbal antics. Their flashing, toothy grins shone out of their unwashed faces like huge glowworms in the murky atmosphere.

The next day, we burnt all our garbage and distributed the remaining food to the herders and to the monks of the Rongbuk Monastery. The truck drivers agreed to take us all the way to the Friendship Bridge between Tibet and Nepal if they were given select items of food. Mr. Li and Louis happily took all the coffee.

The weather was spectacular all the way to Xegar where we stayed in our first barracks hotel. In complete contrast to our trip in, we had to wear dust masks. I swear the dust remained in my lungs until we reached Canada, producing constant hacking fits and a red face that felt ready to explode.

The last view of Everest, from 100 miles away, was heartbreaking. Now that we had recovered somewhat, it was painful to leave without having reached the top. The tortuous roads we had slithered in on were now dry and much safer. Huge hares frolicked in the rocks. We stayed at a friendlier hotel in Xegar than the barracks we stayed at originally. The staff let James and I sample food in the kitchen, a rare privilege. We asked for a bath, not having had one for two months. The hotel owner led us a mile through the dusty town streets full of goat and human kids. He led us into a strange building. It turned out to be a solar heated bathhouse which had been installed by the town council with help from the Chinese. It worked fairly well—we had lukewarm water, and felt glorious—but we were somewhat unnerved when ten friendly men of various ages watched us shower. We never did figure out why. Perhaps it was simple curiosity.

Driving back to the Tibetan border was nerve-racking as the drivers wanted to get home to China. They blasted round the bends 1 500 feet above the Sun Kosi River. Coming round one blind curve, we met another truck. Both drivers slammed on the brakes; they stopped two feet apart. We could hear everybody's heart pounding.

There was no room in the hotel in Zhangmu, although we had prepaid. No surprise. We slept in the so-called ballroom. Food hadn't improved. You could still bounce the rubbery bread off the ceiling.

All the landslides were cleared. We made it through to the heat and fumes of Kathmandhu after filling out, yet again, interminable customs forms. This city lies at a mere 4 000 feet above sea level. We all felt like superman, rushing around all over the place, having dropped 16 000 feet in altitude. We needed the extra energy as there were so many loose ends to tie up from paying extra costs to packing and selling surplus gear to tiny trekking shops which were tucked away in narrow alleyways. Al and I got lost at one point. We fought our way through the crowds and temples until we saw something we recognised. So many brain cells had gone, it was a miracle we found our way back at all.

Our excess baggage would cost thousands of dollars to get out of the airport, but this time we were approached by airport employees. For special considerations, baggage costs could be reduced to $750 US for the airline plus an additional $250 US for the employees.

In Bangkok Airport, James and I took a chance on a seedy-looking hotel on the tourist route. It turned out to be great. We sampled some of Bangkok's magnificent seafood; fourteen courses in fact. The crab claws were as big as tennis balls.

At Vancouver airport, the press were there in full force to welcome us, as was Laurie Skreslet, the first Canadian to climb Everest. It was hard to think straight after all that hardship and uncertainty.

Reverse cultural shock hit. The feel of my lips kissing the hard, somewhat smelly concrete at Vancouver airport made me remember that it was good to be alive. We had overcome obstacles that would probably never crop up again in three lifetimes; we had almost climbed Everest. It was strange that not one of us was particularly disappointed.

The reason was simply that we had already achieved so much. The Canadian Rett Syndrome Association had gained increased immeasurable awareness of the plight of the young victims. As well, I feel we did much to highlight mental disability in general. Research is proceeding full speed ahead at Queen's Hospital in Toronto.

Would I do it again? Yes, but only on a small scale; perhaps a two or three-man team. Knowing what I know now, I could never face those fantastically exciting but mind-blowingly stressful years again. Another project? The 100 000 foot-high volcano called Mons on Mars would be equally challenging, as would swimming round the world underwater. Right now it's great to vanish into the mountains and woods of western Canada, knowing there are no deadlines to meet.

Teams that attempted Everest that summer and fall, the Indians, Brazilians, Belgians, and ourselves, never made it. It was a washout year. Chomolungma, the Goddess Mother of the World, repulsed everyone. Actually, there has never been a successful fall ascent via the Mallory route over the North Col.

$$\bigwedge$$

Everest changed all members of the team irrevocably. After the climb, Alan Norquay took off to see the rest of the East and learned massage in northern Thailand. He now wants to pursue a career in hands-on environmental engineering. John lost his wife and his job. He now has a new girlfriend and his own home construction business. Denis is pursuing his surgeon's career in advanced brain transplant methods while ensconced in Fort St. James, British Columbia. Mario is sitting by a lake somewhere, fishing with a dreamy, detached look in his eyes. Tim worked as a ski operation manager when he first returned, but found the land was too flat. Wanderlust struck him again. James got a promotion, changed his house and car, but kept his marriage intact. Jamie found one of his callings as a disc jockey, using his charm, wit, and repartee. Ernie has a consulting business.

Myk Kurth was last seen pumping gas in Dawson City in the Yukon. His wife, by this time, has a baby Myk. Timo sold everything and took off round the world. Ross became a university advisor. Jim is back in the financial scene in Toronto, the only place outside the Ukraine famous for cabbages. Hilda guides, cooks, and herds sheep north of Kamloops, British Columbia. Mike Sullivan is busy patching up neurological connections in California.

Pat Morrow went off to Antarctica to photograph an amazing environment. Bill Noble moved to Invermere in the interior of British Columbia. Mike Collier is still filming frenetically after the great success of the Everest film.

Alan Hobson gives management seminars but can only use two syllable words in his writing projects. I also conduct management seminars, but I'm really into "cocooning" and writing books. Words over three syllables are a real challenge. ⋀